Perspectives on Non-Sexist Early Childhood Education

Perspectives on Non-Sexist Early Childhood Education

edited by
BARBARA SPRUNG
Director, Non-Sexist
Child Development Project
Women's Action Alliance

Teachers College Press
TEACHERS COLLEGE, COLUMBIA UNIVERSITY
NEW YORK AND LONDON

372.21
C748

DESIGNED BY JOAN STOLIAR

Library of Congress Cataloging in Publication Data

Conference on Non-Sexist Early Childhood Education,
Airlie House, 1976.
Perspectives on non-sexist early childhood education.

Bibliography: p.
1. Education, Preschool—United States—Congresses.
2. Sexism—United States—Congresses. 3. Sex.
discrimination—United States—Congresses. 4. Educational equalization—United States—Congresses.
I. Sprung, Barbara. II. Title.
LB1205.C66   1976   372.21'0973   78-6251
ISBN 0-8077-2547-1

Manufactured in the U.S.A.

ACKNOWLEDGEMENTS

The staff of the Non-Sexist Child Development Project wishes to thank the many individuals, corporations, and foundations who helped make the Conference on Non-Sexist Early Childhood Education possible.

Funds for the conference were provided by grants from the Carnegie Corporation of New York, the ARCA Foundation, the Exxon Corporation, and McGraw-Hill, Inc. We thank them for their encouragement and support.

Contributions of services and materials were made by the Chase Manhattan Bank (Community Development Department), Kenyon and Eckhardt, Inc., Pfizer Incorporated and Sarand, Inc. We thank them all for their interest and generosity.

The Conference on Non-Sexist Early Childhood Education was planned with the assistance of a distinguished committee of early childhood leaders. They came to meetings in New York City from all over the country and gave tirelessly of their time and expertise. They worked on subcommittees to plan the materials display and shared their resources with us in countless ways. The staff of the Non-Sexist Child Development Project sincerely thanks them one and all.

Publicity for the conference was arranged by Public Interest Public Relations, and our special thanks go to Beverly Wettenstein and Andrew Comins for their professional help and good cheer throughout. Also, a very special thank you to Penelope K. Engel, educational consultant, who volunteered her time and expertise as a friend of the Project, and to Irene Tom, Project Secretary, who lettered signs and performed a myriad of extracurricular chores. Our final thank you goes to the staff of the Airlie Foundation whose gracious helpfulness throughout was much appreciated.

Barbara Sprung, Director
Non-Sexist Child Development Project

Felicia George, Project Administrator
Non-Sexist Child Development Project

Contents

7

Parenting

Roundup of Perspectives

Appendices

ADVISORY PLANNING COMMITTEE

Ms. Gloria Primm Brown
Administrative Assistant
Carnegie Corporation

Mr. Brad Chambers
Director, Council on Interracial
Books for Children

Dr. Monroe Cohen
Director of Publications
Editor, *Childhood Education*
Association for Childhood
Education International

Ms. Harriet K. Cuffaro
Graduate Faculty, Bank Street
College of Education

Ms. Emily Davidson
Formerly Regional Specialist
Human Development
Hampden County Extension
Service

Dr. Selma Greenberg
Affirmative Action Officer
Hofstra University

Dr. Nancy Gropper
Research Associate, Agency for
Child Development

Dr. Marcia Guttentag°
Formerly Director, Social
Development Project
Harvard Graduate School of
Education

Ms. Lisa Hunter
Far West Laboratory for
Educational Research and
Development

Dr. Patrick Lee
Program in Early Childhood
Education
Teachers College, Columbia
University

°Dr. Guttentag died suddenly in the fall
of 1977. All of us who worked with her
will sorely miss her both personally and
professionally.

9

Dr. Lilian Katz
Director, ERIC/Early Childhood
   Education

Dr. Jenny Klein
Director, Educational Services
   Administration for Children,
   Youth, and Families

Mr. James A. Levine
Author: *Who Will Raise The
   Children? New Options For
   Fathers (And Mothers)*

Dr. Shirley McCune, Director
Resource Center for Sex Roles in
   Education and Project
Director, Title IX Equity
   Workshops   Project

Ms. Ann Morris
Editorial Director for Early
   Childhood
Scholastic   Magazines

Dr. Renee Queen, Supervisor
Urban School Services, New
   York State Education
   Department

Dr. Teresa Salazar
Associate Director, Early
   Childhood   Project
Education Commission of the
   States

Ms. Joy Simonson
Executive Director, Advisory
   Council of Women's
   Educational Programs

Dr. Marilyn Smith
Executive Director, National
   Association for the Education
   of Young Children

Mr. Theodore Taylor
Executive Director, Day Care and
   Child Development Council of
   America

Ms. Libby Vernon
Early Childhood Education
Texas Education Agency

Ms. Nona Weekes
Director of Supervision and
   Administration Program
Bank Street College of Education

Ms. Frances O. Witt
Special Assistant to the Executive
   Deputy Secretary
Department of Education
Commonwealth of Pennsylvania

PRESENTERS AT THE CONFERENCE ON NON-SEXIST EARLY CHILDHOOD EDUCATION

Toni Cade Bambara
1556 Mayflower Ave., SW
Atlanta, GA 30311

Dr. Joan Bean
Dean, Wheaton College
Norton, MA 02766

Dr. Barbara T. Bowman
Co-Director, Erikson Institute
1525 E. 53rd St.
Chicago, IL 60615

Brad Chambers
Director, Council on Interracial
  Books for Children, Inc.
1841 Broadway
New York, NY 10023

Harriet Cuffaro
Bank Street College of Education
610 W. 112th St.
New York, NY 10025

Emily L. Davidson
Formerly Regional Specialist,
  Human Development
Hampden County Extension
  Office
1499 Memorial Ave.
West Springfield, MA 01089

Enid Davis
1050 Newell Rd.
Palo Alto, CA 94303

Dr. Selma Greenberg
Affirmative Action Officer
Hofstra University
Hempstead, NY 11550

Nancy Gropper
300 W. 108th St.
New York, NY 10025

Dr. Marcia Guttentag
Formerly Director, Social
  Development Project
Harvard Graduate School of
  Education
Appian Way
Cambridge, MA 02138

11

Dr. Roger Hart
Environmental Psychology
  Dept.
CUNY Graduate Division
33 W. 42nd St.
New York, NY 10036

JoAnn Hoit
Director, Mabel Barrett
  Fitzgerald Day Care Center
206 W. 64th St.
New York, NY 10023

Lisa Hunter
Far West Laboratory for
  Educational Research and
  Development
1855 Folsom St.
San Francisco, CA 94103

Anne Gray Kaback
Director, Educational Alliance
  Day Care Center
197 East Broadway
New York, NY 10002

Dr. Lilian Katz
Director, ERIC/Early Childhood
  Education
805 West Pennsylvania Ave.
Urbana, IL 61801

Dr. Jenny Klein
Director, Educational
  Administration for Children,
  Youth, and Families
Office of Child Development
400 Sixth St., SW, Room 5126
Washington, DC 20024

Dr. Patrick Lee
Teachers College, Columbia
  University
Program in Early Childhood
  Education
525 W. 120th St.
New York, NY 10027

James Levine
68 Martin Rd.
Wellesley, MA 02181

Ann Morris
Editorial Director for Early
  Childhood
Scholastic Magazines
50 W. 44th St.
New York, NY 10036

Arline Nash
Director, Early Childhood
  Development Program
Jewish Community Center
1160 Dickinson St.
Springfield, MA 01108

Letty Cottin Pogrebin
33 W. 67th St.
New York, NY 10023

Dr. Renee Queen
1009 Park Ave.
New York, NY 10028

Lyn Reese
1030 Spruce St.
Berkeley, CA 94707

Dr. Helen Rodriguez-Trías
New York Health and Hospitals
   Corporation
Lincoln Hospital
East 141st St. and Concord Ave.
Bronx, NY 10454

Dr. Marilyn Rothenberg
Environmental Psychology
CUNY Graduate Division
33 W. 42nd St.
New York, NY 10036

Dr. David Sadker
Dept. of Teacher Education
The American University
Washington, DC 20016

Dr. Myra Sadker
Director of Elementary
   Education
The American University
Washington, DC 20016

Dr. Lisa Serbin
SUNY at Binghamton
Dept. of Psychology
Binghamton, NY 13901

Libby Vernon
Early Childhood Education
Texas Education Agency
201 E. 11th St.
Austin, TX 78701

Nona Weekes
Director, Early Childhood
   Leadership Program
Bank Street College of Education
610 W. 112th St.
New York, NY 10025

Geraldine Wilson
Project Director, New York
   University
Head Start Regional Training
   Office
239 Greene St., Room 437
New York, NY 10003

Preface

In 1972 the Women's Action Alliance, Inc., launched the Non-Sexist Child Development Project in response to a deluge of mail received during its first months of operation, mail that attested to sex-role stereotyping at the pre-school level. Normally the Alliance staff would have referred the letter writers to groups or individuals who had developed programs around the issue of inquiry. However, since at that time there was virtually no one to whom people could be referred, the Project was created by the Alliance as a programmatic response to their issue.

Over the past several years the Project staff has traveled the length and breadth of the United States talking with parents, teachers, administrators, teacher trainers, researchers, government officials, publishers, early childhood material manufacturers, and others who have been thinking about or working out practical ways to remove the limitations of sex-role stereotyping from the lives of young children.

In 1972 only a handful of people were focusing on the early childhood years as the critical time to begin to address sexism. In October 1976, just a few years later, there was enough interest nationally to call an illustrious Conference on Non-Sexist Early Childhood Education in Airlie House, Airlie, Virginia. In 1972 there were perhaps three classroom items and a few picture books that could be considered non-sexist. Today there are many more toys, photographs, books, and other materials that meet the criteria of being non-sexist and multiracial as well as non-violent, creative, and safe for early childhood programs.

In 1972 there already was a body of literature on sex-role socialization, most of it dated and attesting to the great differences between males and females. Today, many researchers are taking a fresh look at sex differences in the light of the way girls and boys are socialized from birth. They are looking at the role played by pre-school teachers in the sex role socialization of children. They are looking at a new generation of children who are being socialized for equality between the sexes, and they are supplying data from which sensible programmatic change can occur.

In 1972 Title IX of the Education Amendments Act was passed, but no guidelines had yet been issued, and its goal of eliminating sexism in education seemed quite remote. Today Title IX is well on its way to being the major force for change it was intended to be. In addition, Title IV of the Civil Rights Act has been expanded to include sex desegregation as well as racial desegregation, and the Women's Educational Equity Act, which was specifically legislated to promote exactly what its name designates, granted funds to 40 projects in its first year, including three pre-school programs. Clearly the federal government is seriously addressing the issue of educational equity, and many early childhood officials of state and federal agencies attended the Conference.

But, while much *has* happened in the recent past, both to raise consciousness about the existence of sexism in education and to develop concrete programs to begin to combat it, much more remains to be done, particularly at the early childhood level.

Therefore, the aim of the Conference on Non-Sexist Early Childhood Education was twofold: *1)* to share and *2)* to plan ahead. Participants shared information about programs for teacher training, parent education, curriculum development, and materials development. Research and intervention programs were reported on, and several views on non-sexist parenting (fathers and mothers sharing the nurturing and economic responsibilities of family life) were presented. In addition, participants were asked to make recommendations for the future of non-sexist education. The outstanding reports and presentations, representing the diverse views expressed at the Conference, have been selected and edited for this volume so that a wider audience may be informed of the issues involved.

A major goal of the Conference was to provide a forum for discussion; it was the first time the early childhood decision makers had come together nationally on this topic. It is the leaders and practitioners in the field who must decide what steps need to be taken to ensure that pre-school children begin their education free from sexist limitations. A dialogue has commenced, a communication link has been set up, and it is the hope of the Non-Sexist Child Development Project that the following essays will contain information and recommendations of value to readers' community and professional lives and that they will help create a national commitment to non-sexist early childhood education.

Barbara Sprung, Director
Non-Sexist Early Childhood Development Project
Women's Action Alliance
October 1977

Introduction

Ruth Abram
Executive Director
Women's Action Alliance

T HE Women's Action Alliance was established in 1971 to be a clearinghouse for women, women's organizations, and others who wanted to be connected to the resources they needed to develop strong, vital programs that would effectively combat sexism and sex discrimination. It was created in 1971, without staff and without money, but with the recognition of a great idea. In six months' time, a living room, which was then the office, was flooded with 5,000 requests for help from women and women's groups all over this country.

This enormous flood of letters made the staff, which at that time consisted of two people, very aware of the kinds of questions and concerns that women and others were having and feeling. Questions that came up time and time again from women, parents, educators, men, and child psychologists, were: "How do we keep young children from developing the rigidities of sex-role stereotyping? How do we help little boys realize that love, affection, and nurturing are indeed part of the proper role of a man? How do we help little girls realize that the world is theirs to have and to hold? How do we help them in their earliest years make choices that will not one day limit their choices?"

These were the questions the Alliance kept being asked, and in 1971 there were no answers to the questions. So, the Alliance decided that it would try to develop a programmatic response. We searched for a person who could answer the questions and found Barbara Sprung, an early childhood teacher with many years experience. She was finishing her masters degree requirements at the Bank Street College of Education and was looking for a challenging job with a larger scope than a single classroom. We showed her those letters and said to her, "Can you create a non-sexist program that will respond to these questions in a way that has never been done before?" Barbara Sprung replied very calmly, "I would certainly like to try." And try she did.

Her first step was to take herself and a teaching colleague into about 25 very different kinds of centers in New York City. They observed for a entire summer the messages of limitation by sex that were being imparted by teachers and parents. They observed interactions between children and their teachers and amongst children themselves; they looked at the materials, books, and records; and they spoke at length to teachers, parents, and directors in these centers to get their ideas as to what was needed to create a non-sexist environment. After the observation period, a curriculum outline was prepared, and four centers volunteered to participate in a field test that included in-service teacher training, parent education, and the development of new materials and curriculum.

A small staff of three worked with teachers, parents, and children testing the training program, the curriculum ideas, and the materials. Techniques that did not work were discarded. Ideas that worked well became part of the first non-sexist curriculum for teachers of pre-school children, *Non-Sexist Education for Young Children: A Practical Guide* (1975) now utilized by school systems and educators nationally.

During the observation period, teachers and directors responded very enthusiastically to the idea of new materials that would be free of both sexist and racist stereotyping. No one really enjoyed using block accessories that consisted of eight community workers, seven men in a variety of roles and one woman, a nurse. Nor were the family figures—women with babies painted in their arms or aprons painted on their dresses, men in outdated business suits laden down with briefcases, grandma with a mixing bowl, and the like—considered contemporary role models that adequately reflected the family life of day care parents and children. These block accessories, which were unfortunately in my own child's classroom until I pointed them out to her teacher, are but one small example of stereotyped materials children are generally exposed to in preschools.

To correct this, Barbara Sprung went to the major educational materials manufacturers in this country and asked them to produce prototype materials that would reflect no role limitation. The manufacturers looked at their balance sheets and said, "Well, that's a very nice idea, but we're doing all right as we are." And so she did what all good teachers do when they cannot get the materials that they need—she made her own. Handcut wooden figures that did not depict men and/or women in stereotyped jobs or roles, puzzles, lotto games, and other toys that showed the world to children as a place where men and women participated equally were put into each classroom taking part in the field testing of the program.

The materials were so successful in the centers that Ms Sprung went back to the educational materials producers and said, "Look—this is what we were talking about. We're talking about pictures showing men taking care of children. We're talking about families, which can be representative of any child's family, not necessarily mommy and daddy and two carefully groomed children. We're talking about community helpers showing men *and* women doctors, men *and* women nurses, men *and* women construction workers." Three companies took a chance: Instructo-McGraw-Hill, Milton Bradley, and Childcraft. They took a chance, and it paid off. Not only have they produced exciting new materials based on the designs and the visions of this Project, but they began to win awards. Of course they won awards. People were out there, people who wanted materials that did not limit their children.

Today there is a curriculum guide for teachers of preschool children. Today there is an in-service teacher training program for non-sexist early childhood education. Today there is a parent training program. Today there are new materials on the market. Much of this is due to the energy and perseverance of Barbara Sprung—one woman. You who are decision makers are the people with the power to make the decisions that could affect the entire early childhood educational community in this country.

I'm not an educator or a curriculum developer or a materials developer or a trainer of teachers. I'm a feminist, and I'm also a mother. One of the hazards of my job as a speaker on issues of feminism is a highly raised consciousness, which gets in the way of marriage and children. And because of this highly raised consciousness, my husband and I every so often discuss how to make the marriage and the child rearing as non-sexist as possible. There's a steady dose of this in our family with two children. One day not so long ago, I heard my husband say to my then four-year-old daughter, "Anna, tell me, what can't a girl be?" I was terrified. Had she learned her lesson? Did she know the answer? Was she going to fail me at this moment? She looked up and thought for a minute, and her little face expressed some very hard thinking. And then she said, "Oh, daddy, (very defiant) I know something a woman can't be (now I was really terrified). He said, "What's that, Anna?" And she said, "A girl can't be a grandfather."

Speaking as a mother, I don't want educators to crush that kind of perception of self. I want you to help this child fly as high and as far as she can. I don't want ever to walk into my child's classroom again and see those limiting materials I described earlier. I don't want to go to another parents' night and be told that they can't find any men to teach younger children because men don't have the patience. I don't ever again want to hear my daughter come home from school and tell me about the baseball game where the girls stood on the sideline and cheered the boys. I don't want to read another book to my children, which I feel compelled to use as a basis for a discussion of sex-role stereotyping. And it is not just the school environment that I want you to change.

At the grocery store just a few days ago, I was with my not yet two-year-old son. He looked at me and all of a sudden said a word that is much used in our family, "snuggle, snuggle." He stood up in his grocery cart, and he held his hands up. I was so excited, first because he learned a new word, and second, because the word was so loving, so wonderfully loving. I picked him up and hugged him and had that priceless moment that mothers and fathers do have with their children, even if in front of the Campbell soup. Then a man came over and said to my two-year-old, "What are you? Some mama's boy?"

I don't want that to ever happen again. Early childhood educators can help it not happen again. I want a mama's boy, I want a mama's girl, I want a father's boy, and I want a father's girl.

I want help and support in raising a boy who as a man can love freely, who can view women as partners, full and equal, who doesn't feel threatened when confronted with a strong and able woman, and in fact, feels enhanced. I want a man who can offer his children a full measure of affection, warmth, and nurturance. I want help and support in raising a girl who as a woman will be free to realize any intellectual and physical potential she has, a girl who will not ever fear, as you and I have feared sometimes to be ourselves when confronted with the other sex. I want to raise boys and girls who can enjoy friendship and respect for one another.

Together you can create an educational environment that will prepare my children, your children, and maybe even us for the reality of our time.

REFERENCE

Sprung, Barbara. *Non-Sexist Education for Young Children: A Practical Guide*. New York: Citation Press, 1975.

Problems and Conflicts

1

Sexism
and Racism
in Education

Dr. BARBARA T. BOWMAN
Co-Director
Erikson Institute for
Early Education

A CENTRAL issue of our times is the advancement of human rights. A conference on non-sexist-multicultural education is an affirmation of these rights. Depriving individuals of the opportunity for self-fulfillment and denying to society the unique contributions of all its citizens are incalculable losses. The failure to respect, indeed venerate, the biological and cultural differences between people is an enormous waste of human life and potential.

Non-sexist-multicultural education is an attempt to change, through education, the attitudes, behaviors, roles, and functions of groups in society. Its purpose is to support the potential of women and minority groups in our society, to increase their personal development and their contribution to the community. It seeks no less than a change in the social fabric of America—a substantial undertaking.

Social movements are often hampered by the illusions and rhetoric of their advocates. The women's movement and the civil rights movement are no exception. Despite a persistent march forward, both have had periods in which benefits proved illusory and advocated changes restricted freedom instead of expanding it and eroded the quality of life. There have been periods when progress for some was borne on the backs of others, periods when plans failed and friends and allies deserted the cause, periods when programs that promised hope delivered defeat.

The best defense against illusion and self-defeating rhetoric is to keep in touch with reality and to constantly reassess goals and strategies, means and ends. The Women's Action Alliance Conference provided an opportunity for this kind of reflection—a time to hear and to speak, to consider and to plan; a time to exchange illusion and rhetoric for reality and thoughtful analysis.

The exigencies of social action programs frequently leave little time for this kind of deliberation and planning. There is constant temptation to ignore or over-ride conflicts, to oversimplify the complex, to disregard those whose vision is somewhat different. A successful movement must be ready to respond to the ever-changing stream of events, to grasp the decisive moment, to act without debilitating ambivalence. The successful movement must be ready to mobilize energy to act on values.

But action without clear purpose, untempered by realism and understanding, is dangerous. Sober reflection is not an excuse for inaction. It is, rather, a call to act more thoughtfully, to plan more carefully, to increase the probability that when goals are achieved, they will be goals worth achieving.

My remarks are designed to stimulate this process, to raise some issues, to point to some conflicts, to express some ideas and concerns. My intent is to encourage readers to attend to some of the realities we confront, to reconsider some of the hard and complex problems in human and social development, to appreciate the value choices that inevitably accompany social change.

Non-Sexism and Non-Racism: Similarities and Differences

The first point I would make is that non-sexist and a multi-cultural (non-racist) curricula are not the same. They should be drawn up to address different problems and should therefore have different objectives and different tactics.

The belief that sex and race roles are determined by genetic structure, if not by the master plan of God, is very old. Fenelon (Bullough, 1974) said in 1686:

> A woman's intellect is normally more feeble and her curiosity is greater than those of a man . . . It is undesirable to set her to studies which may turn her head. Women should not govern the state nor make war nor enter the sacred ministry. Thus they can dispense with some of the more difficult branches of knowledge which deal with politics, the military art, jurisprudence, philosophy and theology. Even the majority of the mechanical areas are not suitable for them. They are made to exercise in moderation. Their bodies as well as their minds are less strong and robust than those of men.

And a report to the Connecticut Colonization Society in 1828 (Frederickson, 1972) stated:

> In every part of the United States, there is a broad and impassable line of demarcation between every man who has one drop of African blood in his veins, and every other class in the community. The habits, the feelings, all the prejudices of society—prejudices which neither refinement, nor argument, nor education, nor religion itself can subdue—mark the people of color, whether bond or free, as the subjects of a degradation inevitable and incurable. The African in this country belongs by birth to the lowest station in society; and from that station he can never rise, be his talent, his enterprise, his virtues what they may.

In one form or another, the theory of the biological inferiority of certain groups is not new. Biological deficiency has been applied to American Indians, Mexican Americans, the Irish, the people of Appalachia, and the poor as well as to Blacks and women. But the history and traditions of each of these prejudices is quite different. For instance, prejudice against European national groups and Blacks and Indians emanated from different historical events and has been supported by different social structures. John Hope Franklin has pointed out, with considerable eloquence, in his Jefferson lectures (1976) how Blacks have been exposed to systematic exploitation of unparalleled virulence. In this country only Blacks have been exposed to a conspiracy by the church, government, science, business, and schools aimed at depriving them of their human rights. In this country only Native Americans have been exposed to systematic extermination. In the United States racial prejudice and ethnic prejudice, including anti-Semitism, are not identical, and we misunderstand an important reality when we try to equate them. Sex prejudice and race prejudice are not identical. No one ever complains about having a woman in the family!

It is tempting to make simple comparisons and accept simple or simplistic explanations for complex problems. One such simplistic explanation that is currently popular is the inherent exploitiveness of the white male. This kind of explanation is as unconvincing as the "feebleness" of woman's intellect or the "incurable degradation" of blacks.

Race, ethnic, and sex prejudice are complex phenomena, woven in different patterns into the fabric of our society. These prejudices stem from different economic, social, and emotional conditions and events. They differ in intensity, pervasiveness, degree of reality distortion, and extent of emotional charge. Non-sexist and non-racist education are not equivalents any more than are arithmetic and spelling education or gym and reading education. They are all education to be sure, but they do not stress the same knowledge nor do they necessarily teach the same skills.

Whites and non-whites do not live in the same world, and they will not as long as prejudice and the opportunity for discrimination exist. White women and black women are victimized by many of the same practices, but they affect them quite differently because the social context in which they live their lives is different. White women and non-white women, for instance, both receive lower wages than white men, but the white woman is more likely than the non-white to have a white male's assets to add to her own. She is more apt to have alliances with the white power structure than is her non-white counterpart.

Rape is an atrocity to which both white and non-white women are exposed, but it has different meanings, despite the similarity of the act. Susan Brownmiller in her book *Against Our Will* (1976) makes the point that today cross-racial rape is most frequently committed by black men on white women and that some white women are reluctant to prosecute their attackers because they feel the attack symbolically justified. Black women tend not to see attacks on themselves in the same sociological dimensions. It has been suggested that black women often don't report rape because they do not expect anything to be done about it. Underlying the same behavior are different attitudes and, obviously, different self-perceptions. Can the same curricula address itself to girls who experience their sexual importance so differently?

What constitutes a rape? Differing interpretations have historically been used that depend on whether the woman and the assailant are Black or white. Brownmiller dramatizes this point in writing of the Emmet Till case. She says:

> And what of the wolf whistle, Till's "gesture of adolescent bravado?" We are rightly aghast that a whistle could be cause for murder, but we also accept that Emmet Till and J.W. Millam shared something in common. They both understood that the whistle was no small tweet of hubba-hubba or melodious approval for a well-turned ankle. Given the deteriorated situations—she with a pistol in her hand, he scampering back to safety with his buddies—it was a deliberate insult just short of physical assault, a last reminder to Carolyn Bryant that this Black boy, Till, had in mind to possess her.

Correlation of the "wolf whistle" with physical attack is not uncommon when an encounter has taken place between a Black man and a white woman, particularly in the South. The point is simply that even an act as clear as rape cannot escape the distortions derived from the social matrix in which it occurs. How do we educate girls and boys within these different matrix to understand and perceive each other in human and valued ways?

What seems quite clear is that non-sexist, non-racist curricula cannot bolster self-respect and increase freedom without taking into account the different constraints and freedoms that distinguish each group in the society. Curricula that do not fully appreciate the different ways in which groups experience the same or similar challenges will be of little use. The reduction of cultural differences to the level of who eats corn bread, fried bread, popovers, or bagels on Sunday will not root out prejudice and discrimination nor liberate the human spirit.

Do We Need Sex Roles?

The second proposition to which I want to call attention is the relation of sex roles to psycho-sexual development.

Except for the behaviors related to reproduction, there are few differences between the sexes that are determined by natural endowment. Racial differences, particularly in intelligence, are at times hotly contested, but the evidence for such differences between races is equally skimpy. A little more aggressiveness here, a little better visual-spatial perception there, a little better verbal ability or upper chest strength, earlier average age of menses and of walking—these are the slim pickings on which a theory of biologically determined race and sex role differences would have to be built.

If a theory of biological determinism cannot be put forward, then what? Erikson (1968) sums up the developmental position this way:

> Most verifiable sex differences (beyond those instrinsic to sexuality and procreation) establish for each sex only a range of attitudes and attributes which to most of its members "come naturally," that is, are predispositions, predilections, and inclinations. Many of these can, of course, be unlearned or relearned with more or less effort and special talent. This is not to be denied; with ever-increasing choices given her by the grace of technology and enlightment, the question is only how much and which parts of her inborn inclinations the woman of tomorrow will feel is most natural to preserve and cultivate.

Are humans most human, are they to be most valued, when they are as natural as possible? Are humans at their best when they behave in a way that is in keeping with whatever weak instincts and innate tendencies are part of their genetic blueprint? Or are they at their best when they adapt to arbitrary social demands designed to mold them to the environment? Most of us would, of course, vote for something in between. There is no question about the desirability of altering, distorting, or sublimating the seemingly natural tendency toward human aggressiveness, if such social engineering can free us from the violence that is so much a part of our interpersonal relations. By contrast, however, many of us are reluctant to interfere in the equally natural attachment that occurs between mother and child.

The concern of some developmentalists is that interference with the expression of the "predispositions, predilections, and inclinations" may decrease creative functioning, restrict affective expression, and impede learning. The traditional interpretation in early childhood education is that the course of development is blueprinted—weakly to be sure

—and that environmental supports should try to maximize the natural inclination of each phase of development. Psycho-sexual stages, Piagetian stages, life tasks, fundamental needs, and Gesellian norms all assume that there are developmental steps and that these steps require greater or lesser environmental support and stimulation to be actualized. Development as the goal of education has historic roots. Rousseau with his romantic ideals and the Freudians with their biological orientation both envisioned unfettered development.

One of the developmental steps that has been accepted over the years is that of sex-role differentiation. Boys and girls have been seen as having different developmental blueprints and different developmental needs. In preschools, little boys are not asked to sit at the art table as long as girls because their inherently slower development and greater activity level make the art table less pleasurable for them. Shivering little girls in the corner of the play yard are not asked to stay outdoors in the cold as long as the boys because their verbal interactive style does not lend itself to keeping warm.

We have come to recognize that expectations and unconscious teaching contribute to making the block corner more attractive to boys and less available to girls. We have also come to realize that such arbitrary sex-role teaching may unnecessarily restrict the experience of a child and that such restrictions bias the options and alternatives of adulthood.

The acquisition of sex-role characteristics—behaviors, beliefs, and attitudes—is not just a superficial "putting on" of roles. The characteristics learned actually become part of an individual's definition of self, and the equation is formed: "I am because I do and I do because I am." It is part of Erik Erikson's unique contribution to our understanding of human nature that we appreciate the strength and meaning of this tie between individuals and the particular culture pattern in which they grow and to which they adapt. An individual and his or her social experience are rather like two sides of the same coin—one may not have one without the other; both are necessary for self-definition and for identity.

What is it about the sex role that is essential for development? If we are willing to broaden our perspective, we can discard specific practices. Girls can indeed play in the block corner, and boys can do beautiful art work. Because we contend that a particular role or a particular set of practices is inappropriate, it does not follow that children can grow up without any social direction and patterning.

Perhaps I can make my point clearer by making a parallel to language development. Children learn language by abstracting rules from the sea of speech. The rules that a child abstracts eventually lead to adult speech patterns with particular words, sentence structures, and intonations. The developmental potential to learn language has been released by the existence of the language community. It seems to make little difference whether the word a child learns for "child" is *enfant* as in French or *bache* as in Farsi or *niño* as in Spanish. The specific language learned may affect the individual in subtle ways—in how and what is thought—but the critical developmental step of language acquisition is supported. If the same analogy is used for sex roles, we may say that the specific content of the sex role that a child learns is not terribly important for basic development, although this content will subtly affect how the child experiences his or her sex. The developmental need is for an environment in which there are roles, sex roles included, available for children to learn.

Just as it is the job of the developing ego to search out the language rules that govern communication, children are equally committed to searching out the rules that govern sex roles, or age roles, or any of the other roles they are expected to know. Learning these roles is not just dependent upon a teacher's instruction. A child meets a teacher more than half way, striving to know how to speak, or how to be a child, or how to be a girl or a boy. Where roles are diffuse, ambiguous, or conflicting, it is difficult to develop the skills that help define oneself. It is difficult to achieve the feelings of competence and well being that arise from learning the lessons of one's culture and feeling a valued member of one's community.

The notion of raising children so that all options remain open until such time as children can decide for themselves who and what they want to be ignores the relationship of experience to development. At each step along the road to maturity experiences constrain and free an individual for different kinds of growth. As children try themselves out against the particular role models their community projects, they build identities that are both social and individual.

Sexual identity is learned from the interaction of the biological organism—with its structure and drives—and the social environment.

Biological characteristics are channeled, disciplined, and directed to afford opportunities for satisfaction within a particular social milieu. Sexual identity is not simply a biological fact or recognition of one's biological potential. It is an intricate pattern of learned behavior that organizes the biological drive in the service of the society. There are great differences in sex roles and behaviors around the world, but between the two sexes every culture ordains somewhat different roles, both complementary ones, and mutually supportive ones. Each society uses the biological differences, and the need to affirm that difference, as a factor in the organization of the society.

The sex roles presently accepted may not be appropriate. They can certainly be changed. They probably cannot be eliminated. Society may choose how diffuse and overlapping sex roles will be, but it needs to understand that some role definitions will be more supportive to enduring, heterosexual relations (a necessary underpinning to traditional family arrangements) than others. If the prevailing value in the society continues to focus on the family unit, and not simply on the ability to sexually service one another, then the society must carve out reciprocal roles for men and women. Roles must be designed that lead to complementarity and fulfillment rather than to competitiveness and isolation. This will be a difficult task in the struggle for greater equality in human rights.

Sex Roles and Society

My third point is that sex roles are not independent variables but are dependent on and interwoven with the various institutions of society. Sex roles can be changed without interfering with the attainment of sex-role identity and reciprocal heterosexual relationships. Our society can and should allow much more room for duplication and overlapping in the prerogatives of men and women, girls and boys. But institutional change will be the inevitable companion of significant role change.

Child care is one area where a change in women's roles must affect a social institution. Children are demanding, needing, wanting, requiring, and in a state of almost constant dependence for the first six to eight years. Because of our complex culture, we must provide an extended childhood that protects and teaches children; we must enlist a small group of dedicated adults to provide for the economic, social, and emotional support during a long period of dependence. These are facts. They will not change. How should such needs be met?

The family has traditionally met these needs. First the extended family, more recently the nuclear family, has had the responsibility for providing the support a young child needs. The mother was considered the person best able to perform the nurturing tasks.

The deep attachment between mother and child—partly biological but largely socially induced—motivated the mother to perform the demanding tasks of caring for and socializing children in a complex society. Even when the mother was required to work outside the home, most continued to see the maternal role as the primary responsibility of the female parent. The "mothering" motivations and skills did not just develop during pregnancy. Considerable education and training over many years prepared women to carry out the role with gusto and competence. Education for motherhood started at the birth of the girl and was carefully orchestrated.

If the female has had to learn the nurturing role, the male parent has had to provide the economic support required for the 20 to 30 years in which the typical family had child rearing responsibilities. Even more important, the father had to be educated to enjoy the economic dependence of the mother and children. Becoming competent in one's work or achieving success in one's profession often required long periods of single minded dedication. For others, providing an economic base for the family required long hours away from the home. The education of the father was equally arduous, and the role usually precluded day-to-day child rearing.

Today, sharing responsibilities for the traditional maternal and paternal functions is the alternative most frequently advocated. Although this alternative is often feasible, frequently it is not. The values and skills that make an effective "mother" do not necessarily make an effective wage earner and vice versa.

It may be that our society could profit from less of the Puritan work ethic and more of the people priorities that women have been encouraged to develop. Unfortunately, there is very little evidence that Americans are willing to decrease their material orientation for such humanistic goals, little evidence that employers are prepared to accept workers who are child-centered as opposed to work-centered.

There are problems with the traditional model of two-parent responsibility for young children. Indeed, as more and more mothers enter the work force, we are increasingly aware that the two-parent system may have already broken down. But it is undeniable that one parent has a difficult time providing for children. This is indicated by the numbers of children in poverty from single-parent homes, in mental health and delinquency institutions, and given up for placement after the first two or four years of life. All statistics indicate that both the old family and the new family are failing.

We have a number of choices. We can apply ourselves to the regeneration of the old nuclear family system with society furnishing the economic support role when necessary. Such a system would educate girls (or boys) to the importance and satisfaction of the traditional maternal role, and public assistance would provide income for those women (and men) who have no partner. This will require a dramatic change in attitude about child welfare expenditures. The history of welfare in the United States reveals an unwillingness to provide an adequate economic base for the unemployed single parent and children. The conviction that the family must be responsible for the support of children is deeply ingrained in the American value system.

Another alternative is to scrap the traditional family or at least provide another viable model. Certainly many societies have arrangements that work and work effectively. Children in Israel seem quite healthy and happy on a kibbutz where they are raised in children's houses by nurses or *metepelets*. Although such communal arrangements certainly bring about changes in the personality configurations prevalent in the society, there is no reason to believe that such changes would be offensive to Americans. We should be aware, though, that community based child care requires: 1) commitment of the community to particular goals and life styles, 2) commitment of all adults to the children, and 3) allocation of the material and human resources needed for child rearing. Where these conditions are not met, society has instead the institutional child, the child who has neither roots nor ties, the child who is unable to fit comfortably into society, or, worse, is unable to survive. Adult love and commitment, perhaps irrational love commitment, are required from parent surrogates. It is not being currently provided by day care.

If day care centers are really going to "take up the slack" for parents who cannot or do not choose to meet some of their children's needs, then the centers need to be restructured accordingly. They must take children when they are sick and stay open 24 hours a day, seven days a week. Teachers need to be encouraged "to fall in love" with their kids instead of analyzing their behavior. Teachers are needed who will teach values, not who clarify values. Teachers are needed who care about the children, about the parents, and about the community. We need personalized care of children. Are we prepared to establish such centers?

If we accelerate the trend of encouraging girls to think of careers without providing appropriate child care alternatives, how do we intend to meet children's daily needs? Are we in danger of raising a generation of neglected children? Will child care responsibilities be imposed on the poor and powerless who serve as household help or day care personnel and whose own children are often, as a consequence, inadequately parented? Or are there ways to arrange for both motherhood *and* work achievement? Women (or the caretaker parent) have been singularly unimaginative in their demands for opportunities. They have been too willing to accept the continuous conflict between "mothering" and working on the same terms as men. There are other possibilities: part-time jobs, training or retraining, employment beginning at age 40, or work in the home are just a few.

Stereotypes and Prejudice

My fourth and final point is that sex-role stereotyping does not cause prejudice. In the last few years a great effort has been made in educational programming to weed out sex and racial stereotypes and to replace them with images that reflect more accurately what people really do and feel, images that represent what we would like to be. The assumption has been that the old stereotypes reinforce prejudices and justify discrimination and that new models will reverse the process.

Sex- and race-role stereotyping in books, in songs, and in the media reinforce role-related behavior. Every time a little girl sees mom associated with kitchens, she receives the message: "Women belong in the kitchen." When a little boy sees in a picture book a male doctor being assisted by a female nurse, he gets the message: "Men are bosses, women are assistants." When a black child sees only Bojangles images on television, he understands that society expects him to dance and act happy. When an American Indian hears about the "varmint savage," he knows how little he and his kind are valued. Such images have a circular effect. They buttress the stereotypes that gave rise to the images in the first place.

But sexism and racism are not created by television or books or songs. The media, the books, and the songs only reflect the prevailing values of the community. Images that contradict prevailing values tend to be ignored or denied. Madame Curie, the only person to win the Nobel Prize twice in science, has less impact on the lives of girls than does Mae West. Girls read and enjoy boys' adventure yarns without ever expecting to play hero roles. Generations of children have enjoyed living alone vicariously without expecting to do what Pippi Longstocking did.

Children, and adults too, choose to ignore evidence that cannot be assimilated into their own experience. I am fascinated by the many television commercials that are interracial because advertisers realize the advantage of appealing to as broad an audience as possible with their advertising dollar. I have not heard of any child—black or white—living in their respective ghettos, who has questioned the discrepancy between what is seen on television and what is experienced in his or her own life. The children, along with the rest of us, just ignore the discrepancy. Let me be quite clear—I am not trying to discourage efforts to expand children's horizons through the presentation of *new* role models. I am just cautioning that the opportunity to take on new roles must exist *before*, or at least simultaneously with, the presentation of the new roles if we want them to have an impact on children's thinking.

Actually, I often wonder if some of our efforts to change stereotypes is not just another form of the American game: blame the victim. If poor people would only work, if black people would only read better, if Spanish-speaking people would only speak English, if women would not be so emotional . . . and so we draw up curriculum materials showing mommies and daddies who work instead of malingering on welfare, we show black children running off to the library instead of standing on street corners, we show Spanish-named children mouthing perfect English, and we show women in unemotional and business-like professions. What we refuse to come to grips with is that even if the victims conform to the new stereotypes, others will not stop discriminating against them. The statistics are familiar. When matched for level of education, experience, and all other markers considered relevant, some groups in the society do less well than others.

The height of sexism and racism is the argument that women and minorities only need to act more like white men to get rid of prejudice and discrimination. Men work outside the home; therefore working outside the home is good, and women must hurry to the market place if they want to be valued. Puerto Ricans need to learn English and to be on time; Indians need to move off the reservation. Stereotypes are dangerous because they reinforce society's prejudices for victim and oppressor alike. But stereotypes are most dangerous when we believe that by changing them, prejudice is removed.

If we are sincerely trying to develop a non-sexist, multicultural curriculum, we must attack prejudice itself. We should be more direct in our criticism of the ideas and practices that expose women and minorities to humiliation. But most of all, we must work to change the circumstances that cause the symptoms; we must change the economic, political, and social systems that support prejudice. Curriculum materials, if they are to be effective, must reveal prejudices and the systems that support them, and not just focus on creating more acceptable stereotypes.

Conclusion

My intent has been to raise questions rather than advocate solutions. But there is one principle I would like to recommend to you as pivotal for planning a non-sexist, multicultural curriculum. The principle is *care*—care that in our eagerness to do good, we not cause immeasurable harm; care that we don't needlessly meddle in the lives of people, causing more pain and frustration than we are curing. We must remember that the impact of an experience is not the nature of the experience itself but the way each person perceives it.

It cannot be assumed that the same curriculum will be perceived in the same way by boys and girls, by different ethnic and racial groups, or by any of the various subgroups in our society. As we advocate particular sex roles and functions, as we provide new images and new models, as we inspire or instill in children and parents new ways of viewing the world, let us remember that although many of the old ways are no longer useful and adaptive, some of them may have meanings all out of proportion to our superficial understanding. Groups, all groups, build into their child-rearing patterns the means for balancing the stresses they feel. Through humor, impulsive actions, the arts, interpersonal relationships, and adult models children learn the particular behaviors for coping that their society provides.

Erikson (1963) has said, "There seems to be an intrinsic wisdom, or at any rate an unconscious planfulness, in the seemingly arbitrary varieties of cultural conditioning."

Child rearing resembles a self-fulfilling prophecy. Because the problems of the environment are perceived in a certain way, because certain kinds of responses have brought success and failure in the past, particular child rearing patterns have evolved. And because they were practiced, children grew up perceiving the environment and the resources of individuals in certain ways. Those seeking to change children and their families must first familiarize themselves with the reality seen by these children and their families. As Americans we are diverse, and it is dangerous to see us as a homogenous body sharing the same realities. Robert Levine (1975) gives worthwhile advice when he says, "The past and present benefits of this adaptation must be thoroughly understood before it is ethically appropriate or feasible to advocate change."

REFERENCES

S. Brownmiller, *Against Our Will*. New York: Bantam Books, 1976, p. 273.
V.L. Bullough. *The Subordinate Sex*. Baltimore: Penguin, 1974, p. 272.
E.H. Erikson. *Childhood and Society*. New York: Norton, 1963, p. 73.
———. *Identity—Youth and Crisis*. New York: Norton, 1968, p. 291.
G. Frederickson. *The Black Image in the White Mind*. New York: Harper & Row, 1972, p. 17.
J.H. Franklin. *The Jefferson Lecture*. Chicago, 1976.
R. Levine, "Parental Goals and Cross Cultural View," in *The Family as Educator*, H.J. Leichter, ed. New York: Teachers College Press, 1975, p. 65.

2

Preschool
and the Politics
of Sexism

DR. SELMA GREENBERG
Affirmative Action Officer
Hofstra University

Tʜᴏsᴇ who enjoy travel and have had an opportunity to visit Versailles, the Taj Mahal, the Pyramids, the Pitti Palace, the Roman Forum, or the Acropolis have, if you are practical minded, politically aware, and/or economically astute, probably wondered how earlier societies could have afforded such architectural and artistic marvels, such a commitment of personnel and material.

In our time, far richer in resources, it is with the greatest difficulty that public, and even private, commitments of a much less opulent order can be made. Poor Mayor Drapeau of Montreal will doubtlessly be justifying the expense of the Olympic Stadium for the rest of his life, even as Nelson Rockefeller has been justifying his Albany Mall and World Trade Center. The existence of San Clemente and Key Biscayne, by historical standards rather modest abodes, did much to undermine citizen confidence in the honesty and good intentions of its owner. The Queen of England sent tremors through the institution of monarchy by purchasing a house for her daughter that was judged overly grand by English standards of today but is hardly quite up to Duke level in the England of yesteryear.

How has this all come about? How can heads of states be jeopardized by too great a commitment to real estate? What has happened to pomp, to grandeur, to magnificent obsessions, and magnificent possessions? What historical force now allows ordinary people to resent, to challenge, and finally to prohibit the fruit of their efforts to be absorbed by the whim and extravagances of a few?

Versailles, the Taj Mahal, the Hermitage, the Pyramids, et al owe their existence to a rather simple phenomenon—the exploitation of the many by a powerful few. The notion that ordinary citizens are entitled to benefit, as individuals and as a group, from the fruits of their labor is, as a major social idea and ideal, historically very recent. The very notion of citizen, as the broadly conceived definition we understand it to be, is itself no more than a few hundred years old. The idea that ordinary persons have a right to benefit directly from their own labors and to direct their own existence, as an accepted principle of a sovereign state, is no more than two hundred years old.

But what, perhaps, one does need to be reminded of is a less publicized fact, the fact being that as recently as two hundred years ago, almost all the best trained minds, the most logical, most respected people of all organized societies, accepted and supported the right of the very, very few to profit from the unpaid efforts of the multitudes—the right of very, very few to direct the lives of the many.

Sophisticated minds wove tales of great complexity to prove how right, how proper, and how moral it was to require the vast majority of the people to live and to die to advance the comfort, the prosperity, and the well being of the privileged few. These sophisticated minds served the elite with intellectual energy and effort, as all the others served the elite with more directly practical efforts. Did the few who profited so greatly from the minds and bodies of the many admire, respect, and revere the ordinary folk who so richly benefited them? Not at all! On the contrary, the many ordinary benefactors admired, respected, and revered the few who exploited them, for that is how the ordinary folk had been taught.

From early childhood on, peasants' and workers' children were taught to regard those who would engage them in lifelong exploitation with tolerance, affection, and respect. For admiration, respect, and love were due the exploiters, just as power, money, and sex were. But more tragically, the children of workers and peasants, of ordinary folk, were taught to regard themselves and their peers as of less worth, less value, and less consequence. They were taught this from birth on, through language (Your Majesty, My Lord, Your Excellency, Master), through gestural patterns (bowing, kneeling, kissing rings, hands, feet, tugging forelocks, tipping hats), through observation of the vast differences accorded each, and through the direct instruction of parents, religious leaders, and, if fortunate enough to have them, their teachers. Millions of ordinary children learned to know their place and to love its very restrictions and limitations. They learned to love the people who had limited and restricted them, the noble folk who used all their power to retain that power.

To end this pernicious system required that the many become aware of the true nature of their relationship to the privileged few, that they become conscious of their oppression. They had to come to believe their oppression to be wrong and, lastly and finally, that they had the power to put it right.

I believe that the liberation of the common woman must be seen in exactly the same terms as the liberation of the common man, except for one large difference—that the liberation of women is not only the liberation from the few, but liberation from the many as well. Women's exploitation, like the exploitation of any other group, has existed because that exploitation brought great profit at little cost to the exploiters. The exploitation of women has been more continuous, more pervasive, more intensive than the exploitation of any other group of whom there are records.

From at least the dawn of agriculture (Mary Jane Sherfy believes women have only been oppressed for 4,500 years instead of 5,000— it only feels like 5,000), in almost every level of society, within the structure of the family as well as in the structure of society, women have neither directed their own lives nor profited from their own labor. They have been devalued, defamed, and demeaned. The language they speak excludes them, patterns of behavior depower them, their earliest observations teach them that they are of less worth and consequence than their brothers. And if they are still too slow, too stubborn, or too proud to learn their place from these, then their parents, their religious leaders, and their teachers from earliest childhood on will instruct them in the ways of second-class attitudes, skills, and behavior. They will be trained to be both obedient and obsequious; in short, they will become "good girls." Their brothers will be trained to be domineering and aggressive; in short, they will be "good boys."

Girls' bodies, minds, and spirits grow in an atmosphere too tolerant of ease, too indifferent to the transcending of fears and limitations, too accepting of second-class and second-rate language, thinking, and performance. Boys' bodies, minds, and spirits grow in an atmosphere too intolerant of ease, too unsympathetic to fears and limitations, too rejecting of failure and relaxed standards. Both suffer —one from the early enforced inhibition of movement, growth, and development, the other from the early forced extension of self. The one becomes diffident, too shy, and too passive; the other becomes too brash, too intrusive, and too aggressive—one the raped, the other the raper.

Ideology of Patriarchy

Two years ago I went to China and, as is true of the best kind of traveling experience, I learned far more about my own culture than I could, in 17 days, learn about China's. The Chinese Communists have a formulation about all social thought, which I would ask you at least to consider. They believe all social thought is basically political. Thus, there is no psychology, sociology, economics, or anthropology that does not proceed from a position basically political and that does not in some way support the society's political ideas. My friend, Mary Anne Raywid (she's a philosopher of education), thinks that the word "ideology" expresses that better. But in any case, the theory suggests that all publicly approved thought must fit the social ideology of each society's political orthodoxy.

No matter how objective we think our research and theories are, no matter how logical our conceptual framework, they derive from minds prepared by a social reality to consider certain data significant, certain data insignificant, certain issues central, and certain issues trivial. Indeed, sometimes our politics or ideology have us suspend the need for data (Upon what data do notions like oedipal complex, sibling rivalry, or penis envy rely for either formulation or verification?) or to disregard data that disturbs the socially approved theories. Thus, the evidence that women who score high on the MMPI scale of "femininity," the good girls grown-up, are *more*, rather than less, likely to have menopausal depressions is not widely circulated. This is absolutely counter to the Freudian notion that the women who have accepted their "femininity" will have no trouble growing old. Well, it seems they have a great deal of trouble growing old, and that's just not something that people know about.

The Chinese formulation fits what feminists have discovered to be the reality of school life in America. After extensive searches and researches into the nature of school personnel practices, curricula policies, textbook and material content, and teacher-pupil interaction, the accumulated evidence suggests that educational practices support the social ideology with depressing obedience. Surprisingly, the social ideology the schools support is not democracy but patriarchy. Our schools, particularly our preschools, teach notions of a priori determined sex roles, (one sub-, the other super-ordinate), of gross gender differences, and of differential libidinal drive; they support these notions with enthusiasm generally reserved for far worthier causes, coupled with a vigorous determination to remain unconscious of their harm.

I must stop here and say one thing, because this is where the fighting is going to take place. I believe the notion of sex role is basically fascistic—that is, the notion that one knows what someone else's life has to be like or is limited to include, before a person is even born. I see no difference between sex role and peasant role. For me, the notion that one can tell, and force, or predict is one that I have a very difficult time relating to the notion of choice, democracy, and freedom. And I think what is very interesting about this whole issue is that notions of freedom are very rarely discussed in combination with notions of sex-role development. Freedom is not one of the things that is included.

To understand the ideology of patriarchy, I find it helpful to consider it as being composed of three interlocking myths, myths that become translated into attitudes, behaviors, gestures, and language and thus transmitted (or trans-mythed) amongst members of the same generation and from one generation to the next.

Myth of Opposite Sexes

Consider the myth of female-male as opposite sexes. This myth holds sex is the primary discrimination and that this primary discrimination affects all thoughts, all emotions, all skills, and all attitudes. It is what allows the Pope to give as a reason for disapproving the ordination of women the fact that Christ only selected men as his apostles. Well, as one critic observed, Christ only selected Jews for his apostles, and the Church has not allowed that fact to limit the future ordination of priests. Indeed, the original apostles shared many characteristics—language, place of birth, skin color—*all* of which have been set aside in selecting priests during the historical process.

Why cannot the sex characteristic be set aside? It, of course, *can* be, but not while it is thought to be the most primary human difference. This notion of opposite sex is at the very heart of sex stereotyping. It permits the illusion of believing one knows quite a bit about someone if their sex is known and, conversely, that someone's sex can be predicted from knowing personal characteristics. (Thus a person known as tough, cantankerous, strong, a trailblazer, who coaches, is a newscaster, earns a yearly salary in the six figures, and is a heroic sports figure must be a man. Yes? No. A king—but not a man—Billie Jean. And how about Marion, whose face and form has adorned the screen for 30 years, an outdoorsy type—must be a woman. Yes? No. It's Marion Morrison, better known as John Wayne.)

The notion that the primary discrimination between humans is sex allows us to develop expectations that the world of experience and endeavor is appropriately sex divided. Thus, if females have one set of skills, knowledge, abilities, behaviors, and emotions, men will have another. This myth suggests that the 45 chromosomes females and males share influence them less than the one that is different.

Myth of Male as First Sex

However unfortunate is this myth's influence on human development, when combined with the second myth of patriarchy—the myth of the male as the real human being or number one—we move from simple discrimination to sexism. That is, while the notion of female and male as opposite sexes only suggests differences, when combined with the notion of male as the first sex, the differences between female and male become differences in virtue and value. It becomes simply the case that man's work, man's thought, man's words, and man's activities are automatically more valued, more valuable, and thus more rewarded and rewardable. And thus woman's work, woman's thought, woman's words, and woman's activities are less valued.

It is a notion supported by an incredible monotheistic tradition, which at one and the same time says that God is unpicturable and then says that man, but not woman, was fashioned in his image. When fundamentalist religion's impact on our minds began to fade, it is replaced with what I call fundamentalist psychiatry. In fundamentalist psychiatry man became first, not because he was constructed in God's image but because he was constructed with a penis. He naturally is superior, because it is rather cryptically suggested that women envy him his penis. Penises do quite interesting things, but it seems to me that women's bodies are pretty sensational too—they can reproduce themselves, they can deliver food, and do all kinds of other things. The notion that one would automatically not like one's body is simply not believable. Can you imagine a lioness not liking her body? The whole idea is creepy—so I don't believe it.

Before I go to the third myth, I'll tell the gorilla story. Women are told that the stuff they're supposed to do in life is natural, so they don't need instruction to do it. If a boy is going to be a soldier, they don't say, "Well, men are naturally aggressive, so go out there and do World War III on your own." Instead, they get taken to basic training, they have military academies, they have ROTC, and they have the National Guard. And it isn't said, because people have been fighting for 5,000 years, that men know how to fight. But if one is a woman and has a baby, people say, if she's not a good mother, it's because she didn't get along with her mother, she's conflicted, she has penis envy, she'd really rather be out on the job—we can tell by the way she's dealing with her kid. So that's why I like the gorilla story. . . .

There's a gorilla at the San Diego Zoo who gave birth, and, as we learned to say, she was a bad mother. So they took the first baby away from her. She, it seemed, was not naturally a good mother. She was, however, quite heterosexual and became pregnant again. The staff got together and made the following value judgment. This second child she *would* raise. The veterinarians sat around and they said, "How are we going to make her a good mother?" They couldn't intimidate her into motherhood. They couldn't psychoanalyze her into motherhood. They decided they would *teach* her. Isn't that an interesting idea? So they showed the gorilla movies! And she probably said, "Oh! That's what you do with those little things!" She was fascinated. . . . I swear this story has been told to me as true. Anyway, I get a lot of meaning out of it.

Now, let's think of the male as the real human being for one minute, and I'll take you through the whole notion of height. At the beginning, I said we have no words that separate group differences from differences that are absolute. It goes like this. Men are taller than women; women are shorter than men. This becomes an ideal. All men are supposed to be taller than all women. But it can't be, so we help reality along. All women walk around bending their knees a little. Each individual couple has to give the visual impression of the ideal. Therefore, more marriages are made by height than any other single characteristic. She's too short; he's too tall.

To make sure that we never get the wrong idea, visual messages are sent to us from Hollywood. Now, here is the hilarious part. Actresses, through a very interesting selection process, tend to be taller, because they're often drawn from the world of modeling. Models are taller because the viewer can see more clothes on someone who's bigger—it's a real economic thing. So Hollywood has tall women and run-of-the-mill men spanning all heights. They have to do movies together in close-ups where he *must* appear taller, because the audience will think it's funny if he isn't. So if he is Charles Boyer, he stands on a box, and she, if it's a long scene, works in a trench. Monte Python did a hilarious sequence in which an actress was trudging along in a trench, and the director said, "Get out of the trench!" She replied, "I will not. I'm a star!" So we get the visual. I knew the world had changed when I watched the Academy Awards in 1975, because all the women were taller than the men. Margaux Hemingway is nine feet eight or so; they would have to dig a hole to China to get her to look shorter.

Now comes the mind bend; so far, it's only the visual bend. Women say, "I like to look up to a man." No one ever says the other half of the sentence. Well, if one is looking up, do I have to tell you what the other one is doing? That, for me, I think, is one of the illustrations of what happens. I think what drives feminists crazy is the sense that by perceiving reality differently from others, they feel crazy. There's a lot of research that says that parents feel good about their parenting if they obey society's rules. In the time when all girls were supposed to grow up to be frigid, if parents produced a daughter who had good feelings about sex, they would go around saying, "Where did we go wrong? Where did we go wrong?" Being crazy means that one sees the world differently.

What particularly drives feminists crazy is that this kind of structuring of reality—where people actually dig ditches to give the audience the right view—is seen as natural! The feminists' notion of "get off my neck" is seen as intruding in a natural process. Feminists are told to be careful about changing things. I think that is the sort of reaction that causes a great deal of feminist rage, just thinking of the flip flops that have gone on in our world to make things appear what they are not. Think of the Cinderella tale. It is Cinderella's sisters who are the true women. They are the ones who cut off the toes and heels to conform to the stereotype. Cinderella is perfect, but not many of us are! And most of us are cutting off toes and heels to get into the role. So the suggestion to change that, to let women have size 10 shoes when that is their true shoe size, is seen as restructuring what is natural when they are walking around in size 3 shoes. The whole shoe thing is terrific. Go to an antique shop and look at the shoes that real people wore. If you can see any difference between that and the Chinese binding girls' feet, it's really very hard to understand the difference.

One more example about the bending of reality I think is important is the notion of "gaslighting." Those of you who are mature probably remember the movie *Gaslight* in which a woman was driven crazy by just lowering the jet in the gaslight a little. She said, "There's something flickering around here," and the guy replied, "Oh no, you are imagining it." I think for many of us there's been a flickering all our lives, and every time we say, "Hey, what's going on here? How come I didn't get that? How come he got that? I didn't," they say, "Oh, you are imagining it." We have all been gaslighted out. Other people have to see the flicker with you; you have to *all* know you're being gaslighted together.

Mary Rowe at MIT has a different name for that phenomenon. She calls it "Saturn's rings." She says that Saturn's rings are made up of very minuscule particles and when looked at individually, they can hardly affect anything. However, when they are put together to form rings, they create the environment in which the planet moves. Women's lives are very much like that in many societies where the socialization of women is very direct. They're told exactly that they are second-class citizens, that they are worthless, and so on. In our society, where there is more the gaslighting and the Saturn's rings phenomenon, messages come to them indirectly. Language is one way, and that is the other thing I wanted to discuss.

There's a terrific article (Schultz, 1975) that describes words that once had been neutral or positive to women but became, over time, negative. Words that were neutral or non-sexual become sexualized. One of the interesting words, for example, is tart. Tart was similar to a cookie; but over the years, tart, which used to mean confection and sweetness, came to mean tart in the sense of a whore. Many other words dealing with women have gone through a process of depowering or sexualizing or of negating over time. Think about the word "governess." When Ella Grasso ran for the governor of Connecticut, there were bumper stickers reading, "Does Connecticut need a governess?" Yet when Elizabeth I was Queen of England, she was called governess, and it carried no sense of weakness or silliness. It was seen as entirely appropriate. But you have to understand what happens to a word that is associated not only with women, but with children as well; such a word does not convey in our society the same kind of power as the word "governor." Now you have to, it seems to me, become sensitive to why should not Connecticut need a governess.

Myth of Male Sexual Drives

Which brings me to the third myth, which is the notion, again from religion and psychiatry, that there is a sexual beast class, that men are endowed with enormous libidinal energy that needs release, that they are burdened or gifted (depending on one's point of view and lifestyle), and that they need an enormous amount of energy to control this drive. Since women have, according to this theory, either no sexual energy or a tasteful amount, they are not so burdened with the need to sublimate and, therefore, they are responsible for helping men control themselves. Therefore, if they flash an ankle, an eye, or an elbow, they are releasing this barely suppressed sexual energy, and if they get raped or damaged, it is their own fault. That position—crazy, lunatic, bizarre as it may be—has been written into the laws of rape in New York until recently and is probably still the law of rape in many states.

Because men have this terrible burden, many things happen in society. Women have to stay out of certain places, so they are limited spatially. They're not supposed to be out in the streets at certain hours, so they are limited temporally. They are not supposed to say provocative things, so they are limited linguistically.

But what is more interesting, coupled with the notion of this incredible sexual energy, is the idea that men's sexual needs are very easily turned off. Therefore, if a woman asks for equal pay or if she asks her husband or boy friend to vacuum the living room, she will make him impotent for a year. Now it seems to me, bent as women are in their heads and able to accept all kinds of conflicting views of reality, that this idea is a little hard to accept. If, when $100,000 of a $110,000 athletic budget is spent allowing men to express their barely suppressed sexual needs in basketball, football, and other sports, I think we should also believe that their energy is not so easily turned aside. So, either split the athletic budget or do something to rectify what seems to me to be an absolutely contradictory view of sexuality. One is that it's all over the place and can hardly be controlled; the other is that if women become liberated, who knows what's going to happen to heterosexuality. I take on homosexuality next, so stay with me.

I do not think we live in an heterosexual world; I think we live in an extremely homosexual world. Just think of the sex education courses in the schools where they literally separate children for sex instruction. That's part of their heterosexual development? They all see different movies at different times or the same movies at different times. Most women spend their lives among women; most men spend their time among men. Most men seek their recreational activities with men; women are seen not to be interested in the same things as men. If by heterosexuality is meant some kind of coupling in a missionary position once a week, if that is one's vision of a heterosexual community, then that's what exists at the very most in certain relationships. But if one has a concept of people mingling together, we don't have it. Whether you want it is something else.

There are people who believe that one's body is capable of giving them pleasure, all kinds. It can be stroked, enjoyed, whatever, and people would not be limited either by species or sex for their relaxation of tensions. And there is a notion that heterosexuality is unnatural. We do know, for example, that in Greek society, which lined up sex roles very dramatically, homosexuality was a very accepted way for men to behave and was celebrated as by far the better kind of relationship. So the evidence we have is that severe sex-role separation does not necessarily encourage heterosexuality. However, what it does encourage is something else, and this I'd like you to think about also.

What we have done is set heterosexuality in a war metaphor. For us, sex is very barely separated from aggression and violence. One of the problems in discussing sex is that if one does not discuss it in a clinical language (which is somehow so distasteful), one discusses it in the vernacular, which is all male developed. Thus, women are either forced to feel at ease in a vernacular that does not express their experience at all or to avoid discussion, which I think is very bad for them, because until they can come to terms with sexual language, they will not be able to even suggest an alternative view of considering it. But language has intrusion as its model—the invader-invadee, the notion of penetration, of defloration, and the like—all notions more appropriate to war than love; someone might say from the women's point of view that heterosexual genital relations can be more characterized as engulfment.

Not only sex, but women, too, are seen through a war metaphor, and thus there is the notion that sexuality is heightened when the woman is most victimlike, and that is what gives the rape concept. I want you to think about some of those glorious fairy tales. Sleeping Beauty is asleep. She's not passive; she's dead. Snow White is laid out; she is very attractive lying there dead. Up steps the Prince and kisses her. Now she should get up and call the cops. But anyone who steps into her window and kisses her, presumably, is welcomed—a notion so insane, one gets shivers. But it's insane for both parties. It's insane that this is seen as romantic and is sold as romance.

This is my other great literary allusion. If you have seen *Lovers and Other Strangers*, the woman who played the wife kept saying, "We're equal, we're equal." He said, "Well, I can't do it if we're equal," which is, I think, the issue in heterosexuality. And, of course, that's what it comes down to for women. If the only way heterosexuality can go forward is for women to agree to be subordinate, then they have to ask themselves a very hard question.

Part of the homosexual issue, especially I think for lesbians, is the notion that while there is a great difference between men and women and a difference in power, there really can never be a truly humane, equal relation between the two of them. I think you have to understand that it is their belief that typing of sex roles does not at all encourage heterosexuality. It is the very opposite. To be less serious, if you want someone to help you vacuum, you have to live with a woman, if you're female. It is kind of presumptuous, it seems to me, to look at a three-year-old girl and say that if we keep her out of the block corner, she will grow up to desire a long-term heterosexual relationship. Very few people in America seem to be desiring it under the best of circumstances. I understand if you are married by an Ethical Culture leader, you can take a vow that signs you in for as long as you want, so you can be married for two weeks or for the weekend—none of this "till death do us part." The highest divorce rate occurs among people who have been enormously sexually stereotyped, which takes me to my next to the last point on this.

It is my belief that up to now in the marriage contract (It's hardly my belief; it's the way the contract is written) the exchange has been between woman's sexuality and male's money and support—the availability of the female body in return for support. Only husbands can sue for loss of conjugal rights; it's only recently that women can sue for conjugal rights. Isn't that stunning? If women can reach the point where they can support themselves, if they will no longer set up their children to love papa darling, then men are going to have to get love and affection in the same arena in which women get it, which means that they are going to have to get love for love. A lot of the talents men have not been taught will be absolutely necessary for their emotional survival, because they will not get stroked because they can give money and protection to women. Should women change so that they can support themselves, they will have demands of their own at the emotional level and will not have to trade the emotional support of someone else in return for their own financial support.

What we have now is a care elite, which works like this. Typically, if one is male, if one is 40 or 50, and earns a lot of money, one can absorb an enormous amount of care. He can get a strong, healthy woman to care for him. He can get one as a secretary; he can get one as a wife. If one is a child of a rich family, one can get a lot of care also. If one is poor, if one is blind, if one is old, if one is very sick, she or he can obtain very little care in our society, because all the care is absorbed by people who do not need it. The fact that women spend time, or that anyone spends time, feeding, washing, and clothing perfectly strong, healthy, normal adult children and adult husbands is a practice of insanity, because we are not a society that can guarantee care for all the old and all the very young. Worse than that, people who can't care absorb all the caring efforts. The limited number of carers there are direct most of their caring to the people who need it least; while the people who need it most have very few people around to care for them, because care, like love and affection, goes with money. It is an incredible practice and one that, I think, we have to ask ourselves very tough questions about.

Roles of Educators in Preschools

My final point has to do with the relationship of the preschool. The notion that our job is sex-role socialization is a very difficult one for feminists. You know about the separation of church and state. I think we should have separation of sex role and state, and thus schools. What many younger women and older women are saying is, "Keep your hands off their sex roles. That is really not your business." But more than that, it is a trap, I believe. Many women who have spent their lives in early childhood education are people who don't have trouble with stereotypes. They love children; they're good with children. They have even been brainwashed into thinking their skills are natural. The effect is that they underestimate their own abilities and their own talents; they do not see themselves as particularly gifted or requiring a great deal of reward, but see themselves as just doing something that comes naturally.

But it *isn't* natural. The number of people who are very good with young children is very few. We see it, although we keep denying it. We think we are going to change the situation by hollering about it, or objecting to it, instead of recognizing talent for what it is and recognizing ourselves to be talented, professional people who have skills that are very, very rare. We have accepted the notion that we do things that everyone *should* be able to do—there's only some kind of quirk in them that they can't.

We have also, unfortunately, often been party, I think, to the oppression of mothers. If there is a problem with a child, we are very quick to find fault with the mother's behavior. We have not been there to educate the mother; we have not been there to train the mother, or to help her, and yet we find it easy from our ability point of view, from our talent point of view, to find mothers inadequate. Remember the gorilla momma. I think one of the good things for the early childhood profession is that the feminists are saying, "It's an enormously talented and difficult enterprise that we do. It requires skills that most people do not have or are interested in developing." We have to reassess the notion that what we do is easy, that anyone could do it if they only either tried or had not been failed by their mothers. I think in earlier societies one of the things that used to happen when children lived with lots of adults was that they would naturally gravitate to the adult who was good with children. We have selected those people out and made them professional. I urge you to reconsider yourself in terms of that kind of specialty.

One of the things that is very interesting is the concept of young men in early childhood education. I think that it is a bad idea to bring in people who do not do well with children just because they happened to be a sex you're looking for. I think, however, what we want is for the word to go out that men and women both, who are talented and interested in children, are welcomed in early childhood. We also want it known that it's a profession that is to be as highly valued and given the same kind of status as being an internist. We have to understand that the profession is devalued because women are in it, and as women demand for themselves greater value, they will attain it.

It is often said that men will benefit from the women's liberation movement. Now, I never tried to sell that idea, and I'll tell you why. I think those benefits they will get are often those benefits they have been brought up to despise. If what they get out of liberation is more emotional choices and a more relaxed environment, that is not necessarily what they might want or have been trained to want. They are going to have to give up an unequal access to resources, something they have been trained to want.

The other popular notion is that everyone is for liberation—for human liberation. That's part of the idea that the women's issue is too narrow a focus since it only affects a little more than half the population of the world. Women have a very difficult time fighting that concept, but I want to call your attention to the fact that in all of the boycotts we hear about—avoiding countries that don't practice human rights and don't promote human liberties—nothing is said about countries where women do not vote, where women are not permitted to drive, or where women wear the veil. The concept of human liberties is still tied to how males are treated in relation to power.

On the night before the Jewish holiday of Yom Kippur, the holiest night of the year called Kol Nidre, the Jews say a prayer in which they ask forgiveness. It seems to me that all teachers have sinned also and that we have to ask forgiveness too. We have, in the past, narrowed choices. We taught children a language and strategy of exclusion rather than inclusion. We have limited what they might think about. We have limited many of their opportunities. However, as I think about the whole issue, my belief is that it is in the preschool setting where sex role is emphasized and, therefore, it is the preschool setting that has done enormous damage.

I have also thought of the other side, what the preschool has done that is positive. We were the ones who let them paint those pictures and said, "It is wonderful!" So what did we teach them? We taught them to trust their perceptions, to create and not to copy, to originate and not to conform. We taught them to respect themselves and to respect other people. We taught them to work together and to trust their own sense of reality, rather than the picture of reality another person might give them.

Revolutions are made by young people, so what I say now I direct mainly to older people. I am old for a revolutionary. Believe me, it's difficult. What I sense is a big difference in perception by age. If we older teachers did not always teach our students right, we taught them to sense right from wrong. We taught them to desire to put things right and the belief that they could put things right. We not only taught them that they could march to the sound of a different drummer, we taught them how to drum, and we taught them how to make a drum out of free materials.

So perhaps, then, the medium is the message. We taught them a feeling of self-worth, and for many of us there will be no finer summation of our careers than that many of the girls and women we educated chose controversy rather than conformity, challenge rather than compromise, courage rather than cowardliness, freedom rather than oppression. Thus we have all helped to train a generation of revolutionaries. Isn't that a lovely thought?

I am deeply indebted to Harriet Cuffaro for my statements on research. Her excellent analyses of research and theoretical viewpoints formed chapter 2 in the Women's Action Alliance's *Guide to Non-Sexist Early Childhood Education*. (New York: 1974).

REFERENCE

Schultz, Muriel R. "The Semantic Derogation of Women" in *Language and Sex: Difference and Dominance*, Barrie Thorne and Nancy Henley, eds. Rowley, MA: Newbury House, 1975, pp. 67 f.

3

Teacher Education and Non-Sexist Early Childhood Education

DR. LILIAN G. KATZ
Professor of Early Childhood Education and Director
ERIC Clearinghouse on Early Childhood Education
University of Illinois

RECENT pressures for women's equity and non-sexist education have already had some impact on teacher education institutions. Several different kinds of things seem to be happening. First, there are increasingly conscientious efforts to hire and promote women faculty members. Secondly, programs of women's studies are being offered more widely. Thirdly, teacher educators and others concerned with staff development in early childhood education are providing in-service education to help teachers with both curriculum materials and attitude changes. Fourthly, we are also seeing and encouraging more men to come into early childhood teacher education courses.

At present it looks as though the movement toward non-sexism is enjoying greater success than the movement toward racial equality. Such a trend ought to worry us on two counts. First, we still have so very far to go to achieve racial equality. Secondly, there was a great deal of energy and excitement on the nation's campuses in the late sixties and early seventies for black studies and other work toward improving race relations. These efforts seem to have faded away. The enormous energy required to eliminate both racism and sexism needs sustained attention over a very long period. We should not confuse the excited flurries of activity with real achievement. I also believe that we should be tackling both types of deep-seated discrimination together.

The potential impact of teacher education institutions on sexism in the schools is very limited, at best. There is ample reason to believe that what students learn during their training has only a minor effect upon their subsequent work. Keep in mind that teachers are just like other people; they have the same distribution of attitudes, biases, stereotypes, strengths, and weaknesses all other people do. Most of their socialization into the teaching profession occurs once they are employed. Therefore, whatever resources are available for teacher education, it would seem most useful to deploy the bulk of them in in-service education.

It has been pointed out by Marcia Guttentag (see chapter 5) that a six-week intervention program with non-sexist curriculum materials had noticeable effects upon children's attitudes. We have to be careful in interpreting such findings. The effects may possibly be explained by a Hawthorne phenomenon or by the teachers' enthusiasm. If enthusiasm is at work, we must be careful not to count on it as a way of assuring genuine social change. Enthusiasm wears off. There is something about the nature of teaching that seems to cause teachers to fall back into strong habits. Thus, I believe we have to approach the process of change with the intention to work slowly, but deeply; that takes time.

Another dimension of teacher training is the problem of the status of nurturant roles in our whole society. It is a generally useful assumption that the younger the children one teaches are, the wider the range of their functioning the teacher must assume responsibility for. Thus, when working with young children, e.g. three-, four- and five-year-olds, the more the teacher's role includes nurturant functions. Nurturance is thought to require no special skills or training—just a good heart! When you look at child care and other early childhood programs around the world, you find a universal correlation that the younger the children teachers work with, the less pay, the less training, and the less status they have, and, often, the longer hours they work. I worked in one country in which it was standard practice to identify those who were really skillful with kindergarten children and take them out of kindergartens and move them "up" to work with older children. Thus staff morale and self-respect tends to be low in early childhood programs.

These general social trends also have their impact on teacher trainers. Some with whom I have worked have suggested that they are reluctant to "push" their students because they are going out to such demoralizing jobs after training. There is a subtle way in which they, too, encourage abler students to go "ahead" and acquire training to work with older children.

Another dilemma that teacher educators are caught in is that they are often eager to train their students in "progressive" methods and ideologies. Thus many graduates of teacher education programs leave the institutions ready to set the world right and to improve it in the ways we have been discussing. These graduates cause the receiving school systems to accuse teacher trainers of mal-adapting their students to the real world. If, on the other hand, teacher trainers prepared their graduates to do well what is now being done in most of the nation's schools, they stand accused of not advancing the practice of the profession. I believe this dichotomy accounts for much of the cynicism among professional educators. My own hunch is that we need not be caught between these two extremes. We should try to prepare students to do both —to understand how to adapt to conventional school practice and how to introduce innovative practices gradually as they acquire confidence in themselves and as they inspire the confidence of their colleagues.

I should add another problem that influences policy, namely, sensitivity to parental expectations. Such sensitivity is especially important in day care programs because day care workers can, and often do, have enormous impacts on the young. My guess is that the majority of parents are indifferent to the problems of sexism. Those who are not indifferent probably have strong feelings and probably at opposite ends of the pro-con continuum.

How are teachers to work with them? How are teachers going to be sensitive to parents' feeling without being intimidated by them? One approach would be to help teachers to discover their own feelings first and then help them to understand how parents might feel. In this way we may be able to help teachers to work with parents in open and nondefensive ways. I would add here one caution for teachers: never put children into positions in which meeting your expectations increases their conflicts with their parents' expectations. This is an ethical issue. It seems to me that it would be unethical to increase the likelihood that when children meet your expectations, they are going to be in greater difficulty with their parents.

One final point I would like to make is that the fundamental issues that we are trying to deal with in non-sexist education cannot be resolved on the basis of empirical data, or theory, or facts, or other research knowledge. The fundamental issues here are ideological. By ideological I mean a system of beliefs that we hold most passionately, about which we feel most strongly, and about which we are least certain. To some extent ideologies carry within them a concept of utopia as well. You can always tell when you are dealing with an ideology in a discussion—when someone takes your comments or "facts" personally, then chances are you are touching upon his or her ideological position.

Ideologies are important in most fields, but they are especially important in fields in which the data base is weak. In early childhood education we are inevitably caught in a field in which the data base is weak. It has to be weak for several reasons. First, the immaturity of the organism we are concerned about is difficult to "measure" reliably. Second, since the organism is immature, it is in a state of constant change. Thus we cannot tell whether observed changes are a function of growth or of instrument weakness. Third, the definitive experiments that would resolve some of the most important issues would be unethical, and therefore we cannot do them. For example, there is much concern about the effects of early separation of infants from parents, of the effects of multiple caregivers, and so on. We cannot randomly assign one of these "treatments" to large numbers of infants and assess their effects just for the sake of knowledge. As long as any of us have any reason to believe that something is good for young children, we cannot withhold it from them for the sake of science. Similarly, if we suspect that something is bad for them, we cannot impose it on them just to obtain data. Therefore, we are always in a field in which the data are slippery. This slipperiness creates a vacuum, which in turn is filled by often passionately held ideologies. The question is how do ideologies become modified, changed, and improved in the light of whatever new knowledge is available.

We seem to be in need of a new ideology that contains a fresh conception of the "good life" for all, for both sexes and their offspring to come. It has been suggested earlier that it is no longer possible for any one of us to have the "good life" at the expense of anyone else. Men cannot enjoy life at the expense of women, and vice versa. That seems to me to be the major revolutionary idea of our century. We seem to be in need of a new ideology that incorporates this notion—especially the notion that none of us, men or women, can have the good life at the expense of children.

4

Towards Liberating Toys:
You Are What
You Play

DR. RENEE QUEEN
Supervisor, Urban School Services
New York State Education Department

O NE of the main objectives in the growing awareness of the messages inherent in playthings for young children is predicated on the goal of helping children become what and who they want to be. This necessitates an open view of a society that encourages androgynous human beings who have a compendium of traits ranging on a continuum from assertive and aggressive to nurturing and complacent. This view removes the denotative male at one end of the trait continuum and the female at the other end. Stereotypic sex-role assignments program people and make them feel they must be out of step if they do not conform.

This genderization of the sexes is not to be confused with sexuality. It is vital to differentiate the two before turning attention to materials for it is a pervasive fear, with a resultant sense of discomfort, that condoning or encouraging play with toys that have not been ascribed to their gender will negatively affect the maleness or femaleness of a child. Parents have always felt, subliminally or overtly, that they must nurture "boyness" or "girlness" to avoid later sexual identity problems.

Those who live or work with children need to come to terms with this problem before they can objectively assess the toys and materials they select and the environment they arrange for children's playing-learning-living. Gender is something we should respect in ourselves and take for granted without allowing it to program personality, reactions, choices, or occupational roles. Skewed attitudes toward self and others of the same or other sex hinder our functioning. The choice of who one is and what one wants to be should not be filtered through the sex ascription of traits.

If early childhood people provide an open, encouraging environment with materials that clarify and offer options for children, then they can freely explore who they are, what they are capable of doing well, and what interests them, not what they *should* do or what *should* interest them. Our schools and curricula tend to be content oriented when, instead, the stress should be on attitudes and process. How do children *feel* about what they are doing, playing, or learning? What is happening to them as they work out their social options and not dictated choices?

At the risk of overemphasis, we need to remember that children learn about self, others, and self-other roles within the framework of play. We want them to develop their human potential free of prescribed and proscribed societal dictums. But limiting sex-role typing occurs in too many child development centers with well trained, educationally sophisticated staffs. While in theory and in verbal commitments boys and girls are treated openly, equally, and sensitively in these centers, there is often a hidden agenda that gnaws away at sense of self and nudges nascent sex roles. This agenda is hidden in toys, books, materials, teacher attitudes, and classroom environments.

Sexist Packaging of Toys

Much attention has been paid to children's literature and, as a result, trade and textbook publishers have made strides in changing characterizations, illustrations, and story formats, albeit with a long way to go. The toy market has been slower to respond, often ascribing valid business and production reasons to their lassitude in developing or producing new non-sexist materials. There is little validity, however, for the most common pervasive negativism—that found in the packaging and promoting of the products. Allena Leonard in a Public Action Coalition on Toys (PACT) report states:

> Too many of the available range of toys perpetuate the myth of male superiority by showing boys and boys' interests in a more prominent and positive way than girls and girls' interests. Toys marketed to boys place a high value on action, aggression, skills, and the acquisition of knowledge. Toys marketed for girls carry a different message: charm, a pretty face, espensive clothes, and beauty products that will enable a girl to get married and acquire her own house to clean and baby to cuddle. It's important for her to know how to mix lemonade in a pitcher but not how to mix chemicals in a test tube. In reality, children of both sexes suffer when the scope of their aspirations and imagination is narrowed and only half their development encouraged. Boys lose the chance to develop the quiet and nurturing sides of their personalities, while girls are discouraged from action and achievement.

While I am not maintaining that a toy is a panacea, there is no valid rationale for its package to depict stereotypic behaviors or attitudes. Messages on the boxes tend to preclude open curiosity and dictate usage. In 1975-76 the PACT committee working to select non-sexist, multiracial, safe, nonviolent toys often had to rule out a product because its packaging and description did not meet the goals of equal participation and equal representation. A recent survey of product packaging was encouraging; it was possible to pick out materials that met good packaging criteria. But many new toys that will be purchased, as well as those that abound in classrooms and homes, still convey sexist shibboleths.

To join forces in effecting changes in the toy market's design, description, promotion, and advertising is the ultimate goal. Contiguous with that our task is to design positive approaches to selection and use of materials in our work with children, teachers, prospective teachers, and parents and then to put this in perspective to the framework of play. Play is the vehicle children use to find out about themselves, their world, and their place in it. We cannot dismiss boy-girl dichotomization for it is a behavior determinant that is insidiously present.

Parent Workshops

Research by Ross and Ross, reported in *In All Fairness* (Golden and Hunter, 1974), supports the view that play is increasingly sex-typed in a child's first three years. They found that pre-school boys and girls resist playing with sex-inappropriate toys even when urged to do so by a teacher they wanted to please. Boys were under greater pressure and showed much anxiety after a choice was made for them by a teacher. Children respond to messages about genderized toys from myriad sources—older children, peers, T.V., magazine advertisements, adults, and package illustrations. Since these cues become deterrents to play by age three, efforts to mitigate them need to occur very early through parent education and pressure groups in the media.

An important initial step in confronting messages that are transmitted in play situations is to provide workshops for parents, with guidelines to alert them to criteria for toy selection. Material selection begins with the first mobile when boats, horses, and abstract shapes are selected for boys, but flowers and dolls are chosen for girls. Selection then moves into demonstration. When adults give a doll or stuffed animal to a small girl, they usually demonstrate hugging or nurturing but do not wait to see what she will do with it. If perchance a similar doll *should* be given to a boy, he is allowed to explore its use. Then we witness parental exclamations about a girl's maternal instincts when a child emulates the adult in doll play!

Parent workshops could explore approaches to the use of toys and to the need for more open choices. Certainly a child's tendency to play is innate, but his or her choice of toys and games is the product of the culture —not biology. It is important to stress nonstructured materials, such as large and small blocks, playhouses, games, and toys that encourage open-ended family and occupational roles. Parent workshops can produce puzzles and lotto games in the manner described in Barbara Sprung's book (1975). Parents can be encouraged to make or ferret out dress-up clothes that are not frilly, easy to put on, and appealing to both boys and girls. Encourage them to bring in all kinds of hats, which evoke a role and are fun to wear.

As you alert parents, you also develop insights into your own attitudes and evaluate your school environment. Observe play patterns and keep a checklist of children's choices and activities to see who spends time within the playhouse, the block corner, woodworking, creative art, manipulative, and cooking areas. With this information plan group discussion of the various areas. Take small groups of children on play tours so they can try out unfamiliar materials and areas. Teachers' involvement will encourage timid girls to play with blocks and boys to find nurturant roles in the house corner. Try to introduce toys in categories that individual children eschew and keep records of their reactions. To reroute play interests teachers need to conduct mini-studies with follow-up activities.

Avoiding Sexism in the Curriculum

In assessing materials the curriculum is confronted. Many materials are available that provide activities and extend information for the trips teachers take with children and the concepts they help them to develop. If available materials do not completely meet the non-sexist criteria, but there are no other products that tie in with the curriculum concepts or goals, you can either adapt them to your own design or use their negative aspects as springboards for discussion. You have to tread lightly here; you are caught between Scylla and Charybdis—the Scylla of using materials that compromise non-sexist principles, the Charybdis of feeling guilty about not meeting the children's educational needs.

The decision is easier if it is the packaging that is sexist. Remove the box and place the materials in a neutral container. If brooms, mops, and housekeeping equipment are placed in a neutral area ready for use, both sexes will incorporate these items into their dramatic play. Games with many pieces or parts can be placed in plastic boxes with teacher-made signs or illustrations placed on the containers. It is a good idea to design posters or select photographs depicting men and women sharing tasks to decorate play areas.

In the overall world of playthings, a survey indicated that girls are offered an abundance of toys that stress domesticity and seductiveness, witness "Suzy Homemaker Oven," "Barbie Dolls," and Cher with a mannequin wardrobe. Boys' toys offer more options—trains, trucks, and other motor vehicles and toys with moveable parts that encourage manipulation, construction, and control. Toys geared to girls are not made to be explored or taken apart; the stress is on quiet passivity in contrast to active play. These gender-directed toys transmit not merely subtle cues but bombastic messages.

Parents and teachers have become aware of the need for opening options through curricula revisions, non-sexist literature, and dolls for boys, but this is palpably insufficient in light of the reaction of very young children—boys who refuse to play with a "girl's toy!" and girls who are forced to suppress interest in male-oriented toys. There is spillover to developmental concerns, for affective and intellectual growth depend on open-ended encounters with playthings and people in nurturing person-caring environments.

This is illustrated in active play areas. Active play toys, since they are nonstructured and therefore non-sexist in design, are often omitted when considering sexist materials, but they present a real problem since sexism is ascribed to them by playing expectations and patterns. The limited role of such toys in the play lives of girls is related to their environmental competence as studied and reported by Roger Hart (1976). He found that parental attitudes restricted environmental exploration and boundaries, resulting in timid use of active toys by females. Spatial exploration and manipulation of the environment are essential since through them spatial ability tasks are learned, which are an integral part of all evaluative intelligence and ability tests and can be generalized to other types of problem solving.

Girls who are timid about big muscle activities need to be stimulated and supported in trying to do them until they develop confidence. Manipulative toys should be set out and introduced to both sexes to encourage sharing them. We should make available construction and large muscle activities for *all* children to experience—girls as well as boys.

Most early childhood centers consider the housekeeping area *de rigeur* and expect it to be the bailiwick of the girls. We can no longer smile indulgently with a covert awareness that "girls will be girls." If societal expectations are to be expanded to include males as well as females in domestic and nurturing roles and females as well as males in nontraditional career roles, children need to be encouraged to try these widely varied roles beginning in their early years.

Boy and girl dolls representing multiracial groups need to be anatomically correct and wear realistic clothing. Cardboard dolls with an assortment of clothes should be available for block play or play houses. The variety and proliferation of dolls will say to the children, "Playing with dolls is fun. There are dolls that look like you, and dolls that look like your friends. We expect you to try out new ideas and roles." Accessories that require motoric involvement, such as trucks, cars, or planes, extend and remove sexist connotations from the doll play area.

All of us involved in early childhood are conversant with the function and value of play in children's language, social, emotional, intellectual, and physical development. It is a way of learning adult roles and expectations, of discovering and exploring the material world, of developing insights into covert and overt signals, a stage for enhancing self-concept, and a dynamic way of learning, refining judgments, and solving problems. Benjamin Bloom posits that the period of most rapid growth in learning achievement and growth in certain personality traits occurs during the time encompassed by infancy, toddlerhood, nursery school, and kindergarten—when children are playing not studying.

> By the time children go to elementary school, some of the most important things that ever happen to them are already behind them (Kaplan, 1974).

If toys, materials, and games are the tools of play, then clear logic necessitates introspection and circumspection in selecting these tools. If we can act to remove anything that mitigates against reaching human potential, as sexist materials do, then we are so charged.

REFERENCES

Golden, Gloria, and Hunter, Lisa. *In All Fairness: A Handbook on Sex Role Bias in Schools*. San Francisco: The Far West Laboratory for Educational Research and Development, 1974.

Kaplan, Frank and Kaplan. "This Issue," *Theory into Practice*, Vol. XIII, No. 4, October 1974, pp. 239-243.

Leonard, Allena. *Toy Selection*. New York: Public Action Coalition on Toys, 38 W. 9th Street, n.d., mimeo., p. 4.

Saegert, Susan, and Hart, Roger. *The Development of Environmental Competence in Girls and Boys*, New York: Department of Environmental Pyschology, The Graduate School and University Center of the City University of New York, 1976.

Sprung, Barbara, *Non-Sexist Education for Young Children: A Practical Guide*, New York: Citation Press, 1975.

Research
Overviews

5

The Social Psychology of Sex-Role Intervention

DR. MARCIA GUTTENTAG
Formerly Director, Social Development
Project
Harvard Graduate School of Education

I BRING an optimistic message, a hopeful one, but a differentiated one based on research findings. I want to report on a large-scale study my colleagues and I conducted using a non-sexist curriculum intervention in the schools. The purpose of our intervention was to stimulate non-sexist thinking by boys and girls in three major areas: jobs and occupations, family roles, and socio-emotional roles.

The Methodology

Children in three different age groups participated in the study—kindergarten and grades five and nine. The three age groups were selected as representative of the different cognitive stages defined by Jean Piaget—preoperational, operational, and formal operational. We wanted to find out whether children's levels of thinking would in any way influence their reaction to the non-sexist intervention.

The children were in three different school systems that provided a range of social class, from lower-lower class to very upper-middle class and, to some extent, upper class. The children were all white and were of diverse ethnic background, including large subsamples of Italian, Portuguese, Jewish, Irish, and Spanish-speaking children. Overall, more than four hundred children were involved in the study.

We used a Solomon Four-Group Design. In such a design there is a standard control group that receives pre-testing and post-testing but no intervention, a second control group that receives post-testing only, a standard experimental group that receives the intervention and both pre- and post-testing, and a second experimental group that receives the intervention and post-testing. This type of experimental design allows researchers to determine if there are any effects associated with pre-testing and if there are any ripple effects in the same school, for instance, that a child who wasn't in the experimental group still shows some of the effects of the intervention.

Available measures of sex-role stereotyping were inadequate for our purposes. For one thing, many of them are forced choice measures, that is, the test requires children to choose between either a sexist or non-sexist response or between a masculine and feminine response. This type of measure is worthless because it does not give children enough range of possibility in what they can say. The measure essentially forces a child to say what the tester has already defined as the possible alternatives.

Secondly, there are almost no measures that are truly developmental in nature and permit longitudinal or cross-age comparisons. The measures used with kindergartners are totally different from those used with fifth graders, and one has no way of knowing whether what is found with kindergartners is in any way comparable to what is found with fifth graders.

What we did was to develop a large number of our own measures, which were comparable across ages and were open ended, so that the children could tell us about their experiences in their own words and not in our predetermined categories. For example, one measure, called the Typical Day Measure, asked children to tell us what a typical day would be like for them when they were grown up and 30 years old. After they told us their stories, we asked a lot of questions that were oriented toward non-stereotyped family roles, non-stereotyped job roles, and non-stereotyped socio-emotional roles: "What if you wanted to go to work? What would happen? What if you stayed home? What would happen?" Then we asked them to describe a typical day for a grown-up man and a typical day for a grown-up woman.

We had the children generate adjectives about what men and women were like and then asked them to tell us stories using the opposite sex for the adjectives that they had generated. If they gave us a list of words that described a boy, we then asked them to use those same words to tell a story about a girl.

We also used a modified semantic differential based on children's own language. A semantic differential is simply a set of scales with two polar extremes and some choices in between. We chose stereotyped and non-stereotyped adjectives and many neutral adjectives. Children were asked to use the scales to describe ideal boys, ideal girls, real girls, real boys, and themselves.

The intervention can best be characterized as a "kitchen sink" intervention. When you work in a field setting, you want to throw in everything that is possible to maximize the power of the intervention. This is quite different from a laboratory study in which one carefully controls all variables except the independent one that is manipulated. We had a curriculum staff who designed a non-sexist curriculum in English and social studies. We had wanted to cover math and science as well, but there simply are not enough non-sexist materials currently available in those areas. On the other hand, a good deal of non-sexist material has been produced for English and social studies. For a complete description of the materials used, I refer you to my book *Undoing Sex Stereotypes* (1976), which covers the curriculum in detail.

We conducted teacher training sessions in which we discussed research on sexism in the schools and on the effects of differential teacher behaviors with boys and girls. We explained everything we were doing and why we were doing it. In special sessions we trained the teachers to interact with children in a non-sexist way. There was at least one male teacher at each grade level except kindergarten.

We also enlisted the children's peer groups in this study. With the current federal regulations on doing research in schools, one must tell the children and their parents what you are doing; otherwise you can't do the study. We tried to use this to our advantage by telling the children at every grade level in their own terms what we were doing and why we were doing it; then we asked them to help each other in helping us to do it.

Briefly, the objective of our intervention was to stimulate psychological androgyny. We define androgyny as opening up a variety of flexible possibilities for both boys and girls in three major areas—jobs and occupations, family roles, and socio-emotional roles. In large part, the intervention involved presenting a variety of different possibilities for both boys and girls in these three areas. The intervention lasted for six weeks. During that time we observed what happened in all the classrooms participating in the intervention study.

The Findings

At the start we checked to see if there were differences in children's sex-role attributions that were related to differences in social class, in ethnic background, and whether or not their mothers worked: in short, there were no differences. In other words, it didn't matter if a child was growing up in an Italian or Irish home; they all knew the stereotypes, and they all knew the *same* stereotypes. It didn't matter if the mother was working in a low status or a high status job or whether she was working at all. The children still knew the stereotypes. It seems that the distinctive ethnic and social class variables to which these children had been exposed in their homes were nowhere near as powerful as the society-wide stereotypes about sex roles.

Let me mention, however, that there *was* one effect for the employed mothers. Boys who had employed mothers—boys in the fifth and ninth grades—became more stereotyped following the intervention if their mothers were employed. This seems puzzling, but we think that what happened was that the peer groups and the content of the intervention alerted these boys, in a way they had not been alerted before, to the fact that a working mother did not fit the stereotype. It made the issue much more visible for them; and, the ninth-grade boys especially became more sexist as a result of the intervention.

Let me summarize what each group of children were like before the intervention and what happened to them after the intervention. Before intervention kindergarten boys and girls very strongly believed that males and females do different things and they very seldom have the same jobs. They saw men in strictly traditional male jobs and many of them low in status, such as postmen and policemen—the kinds of things depicted in children's books. Women's roles were predominantly interpersonal in nature. There was little overlap between the occupational roles ascribed to the two sexes. The kindergartners could clearly describe personality stereotypes of girls, but they were less sure about the masculine stereotypes of boys. When describing themselves, both the boys and girls chose desirable characteristics that crossed stereotyped lines. That is, both the boys and girls believed that they were strong, obedient, attractive, and the like.

In the post-intervention we found that the kindergartners, both boys and girls, very significantly changed their attitudes about occupational possibilities for men and women. On the job lists (a measure that asked children to generate jobs men and women could have), they offered equivalent numbers of jobs for both sexes. They reduced the numbers of jobs that they thought were restricted to one sex or the other and dramatically increased the proportion of jobs they believed could be held by both sexes. They also significantly increased the number of high status jobs that they thought might be available to women and decreased the number of jobs solely interpersonal in nature that they thought women could hold.

While the intervention had a very great effect on expanding their beliefs about job and occupational possibilities, the children's stereotyping in the socio-emotional sphere was unchanged. However, what was very interesting is that they were totally unstereotyped in their ideas about what they themselves were like, and they became much less stereotyped than other children. They dropped whatever stereotypes they had about what all boys are like and what all girls are like, and they became much freer about socio-emotional possibilities for other children.

The fifth graders were the least stereotyped group at the beginning. They showed considerable diversity of opinion initially about what is appropriately or inappropriately stereotypical for men and women. They did not make very many discriminations between men and women in societal or occupational roles. However, when further questioned about their choice of a nontraditional position for a woman, for example, they were quick to recant or to disavow a woman's occupational roles. In other words, although they were perfectly willing to conceive of less stereotyped roles, they were not firmly convinced and could be easily dissuaded. The fifth graders, although very open to great diversity, apparently were not receiving much support for holding these ideas and would readily drop them.

The fifth graders, both boys and girls, were extremely interested in justice, equality, and rights. They talked about fair employment practices for both sexes. Despite that, they believed that girls were better in interpersonal jobs and that men were more likely to continue to have jobs in fields that they had traditionally dominated.

What was most interesting about the fifth graders, who were very non-sexist in their occupational attitudes, was that they were extremely sexist about family roles, especially in their descriptions of leisure time activities. The men played golf and read newspapers, while the women kaffee klatched; no men ever kaffee klatched. It would appear that before the intervention children of this age were at least aware of what was going on in society in terms of occupational change, but there still existed an untapped area in their ideas about family roles, which had essentially not been influenced by changes in the culture.

Interestingly, each sex actively stereotyped the opposite sex more strongly than its own sex. Children were the least stereotyped about themselves as individuals, they were more stereotyped about their own sex, and they were most stereotyped about the other sex. This was true for both sexes, but the boys were much more stereotyped about what girls could be and do than the girls were about boys.

After intervention the fifth graders changed dramatically; they became extremely non-sexist. The intervention had a great effect on whatever occupational stereotypes they had. There was less of an effect on family roles, although there was some; the least effect was on socio-emotional roles. Throughout the study the girls changed greatly, and when the boys changed, they always changed somewhat less than the girls.

The ninth graders really surprised us. They were not at all concerned with issues of justice and fairness and rightness. In fact, the ninth graders, expecially ninth-grade boys, were the most stereotyped of any of the children in the study. Before the intervention, we found the girls believed that ideal women should be beautiful and very socially acceptable, but that they, themselves, each individual girl, were below the norm in attractiveness and in social acceptability. The boys, on the other hand, each privately thought that they were above the norm in social acceptability, attractiveness, and strength. Thus, by the ninth grade, all that positive sense of self that we observed in the kindergartners and the fifth graders had disappeared for girls. The girls were very much concerned with a number of issues before the intervention, such as how it is possible to combine family and a career. Some of the stories told by girls were quite realistic in their treatment of the problems they perceived in trying to integrate the two, whereas in the boys' stories, there was very little discussion of any problems that could not be overcome.

The intervention had very powerful effects on the ninth-grade girls. Even though we had done nothing in particular to include material on attractiveness or social desirability, the ninth-grade girls changed very radically in their self concepts. They saw themselves as at the norm or sometimes above it in terms of social attractiveness and desirability. These girls also changed greatly in the number of occupational choices that they thought were possible for women and in their ideas of family roles. What particularly changed was that they became less troubled. They gave less failure-ridden answers to questions about the combination of family and career. The girls' attitudes were significantly altered by the intervention, and these changes occurred in areas that we had not directly targeted in our intervention.

The ninth-grade boys contrasted completely to the ninth-grade girls. Overall, the boys became more stereotyped following the intervention. We think that this is related to the effect of the peer group. The intervention made these issues salient to the peer group's thinking on sex roles, and the peer group then exerted considerable conformity pressure on the boys to be, one might say, more macho than they were.

This sounds like a sad ending, and as I promised a happy ending, let me now report this. We independently ranked the teachers in this study. We had someone who knew nothing whatever about the hypotheses of the study come in and observe the teachers in the classrooms. The teachers were ranked according to how enthusiastic they were about the intervention and the extent to which they actually implemented all of the materials. Interestingly, the top-ranked teacher in the study was a ninth-grade teacher. We found that in her classroom, which we know was absolutely no different from any other classroom before the study, both girls *and* boys changed very significantly in the direction of non-stereotyping in all three areas. In fact, the rank of this teacher, that is, her enthusiasm and her use of materials, almost perfectly predicted how much her class changed. Thus, even at the ninth-grade level, where teachers were essentially bucking the peer groups of boys, if a teacher was enthusiastic in her or his use of the materials, she or he was able to move the entire class in the direction of non-stereotyping. I believe that's a very hopeful finding, because it's clear that to effect change, a teacher must essentially oppose the influence of the boys' peer group.

Summary

To summarize, what we were dealing with was an overall sex stereotype that these children had learned through media, literature, and their peer groups; what their mothers were like and the kinds of families they came from were relatively less important. Second, I think we've seen that an intensive intervention, even one for only six weeks, had really dramatic effects on the attitudes of a great many children. A word of caution though—we do not know how long-lasting these effects were. The most dramatic were on the girls; the boys changed the least, although there was change in kindergarteners and fifth graders. Third, we learned that teachers are a critical element in change and that very enthusiastic and skillful teachers could change even ninth-grade boys.

To conclude on a hopeful note, it seems that a non-sexist curricular intervention can have great impact at all three age levels, but we need to concentrate much more than we have been on ways to change boys' stereotyping.

REFERENCE

Guttentag, M, and Bray, H. *Undoing Sex Stereotypes: Research and Resources for Educators.* New York: McGraw-Hill, 1976.

6

Teachers, Peers, and Play Preferences: An Environmental Approach to Sex Typing in the Preschool

Dr. LISA A. SERBIN

Assistant Professor of Psychology and Co-Director
Butternut Hill Preschool, State University of New York at Binghamton

IN every classroom there is an unofficial curriculum, a part of the learning experience that is determined by the teacher's attitudes and behavior rather than by a formal syllabus. In regard to sex typing, much of this unofficial curriculum is "hidden;" teachers themselves are often unaware of their own expectations and behaviors that effectively sustain and reinforce conformity to sex-role stereotypes.

The research in which my colleagues and I have been engaged for the past five years has focused on differences in the educational experiences of boys and girls during the preschool period. By observing the actual daily process of classroom learning, we have attempted to describe the different ways in which boys and girls receive attention and instruction and the different ways they are taught to behave in learning situations. We have also tried to determine objectively the consequences of these differential experiences, and, finally, to develop effective programs for reversing sex-stereotyped behavior patterns that had previously been maintained in the preschool environment. I am going to summarize some of the results of our research and to describe the implications of these findings for classroom programs.

I personally became interested in preschool sex stereotyping after an experience I had when I was a graduate student. In 1971 I was observing a nursery school in New York City. It was around Easter time, and the teachers were having an Easter celebration with the children. I watched during music time, and the first thing I saw was the teacher asking the little boys to stand up while "Here Comes Peter Cottontail" was played on the piano. All the boys were bunnies. They hopped all over the room. After the boys had had their turn and had all been Peter Rabbit, they sat down, and then it was the girls' turn.

This time the teacher played the Easter Parade song, "In your Easter bonnet . . ." The girls paraded around the room. At the end, the teacher at the piano stood up and looked very solemn. She said, "Ladies, that isn't the way we have a parade. When we have a parade, we all walk very nicely, and we pick up our feet so we don't make lots of noise on the floor, and we all walk like little ladies. Now let's do it again." She sat down and played "In Your Easter Bonnet" again, and the little girls went very quietly tiptoeing around the room. Then they sat down.

A little boy raised his hand and said, "The girls got to go twice. Don't we get to go twice?" The teacher sat down at the piano and played "Here Comes Peter Cottontail." The boys hopped all over the room and made quite a good bit of noise, but nobody said anything to them about being "gentlemanly" or quiet or making "nicely" restrained movements.

This little incident bored into my head over the next weeks and months. I started thinking to myself, what are these children learning? Is this something pervasive or was it just a quirk of this particular teacher? It seemed to me that if this was a pervasive aspect of the preschool curriculum, something different was being taught to boys and girls, something about what is expected of them. Girls were being taught to restrain their movments, boys were encouraged to use their large muscles and move around freely. And I thought, maybe this is pervasive. Maybe it doesn't just affect how they behave when they have music time; maybe it goes on beyond this.

About this time I started my internship. I'm a clinical psychologist.

I did my internship at a county mental health clinic, and there I noticed something very odd. Among the children five times as many boys as girls were being referred for psychological problems. The most frequent reason for referring these children was some kind of disruptive or aggressive behavior. In most cases a teacher was the original source of referral and had complained that a child was unmanageable and/or inattentive in class. Ultimately the child was sent to the clinic.

The other thing I noticed that seemed very odd was that my adolescent and adult caseload was very different. Instead of seeing primarily males at these ages, we were seeing females. Females outnumbered males by about three to one in the adolescent and adult caseload. I wondered why there was a "flip flop" at about age 13 or 14. In all of my clinical training nobody had ever pointed out this phenomenon. I wondered if it was a fluke of our particular clinic, but when I looked at the statistics, I found that the same phenomenon exists nationwide.

The incident at the nursery school came back to me at that point. I wondered if there was something about the socialization boys and girls receive that results in these differences in psychological and emotional difficulties. I certainly wasn't naive enough to think that the nursery school was the primary source responsible for this, but I thought, "Maybe there's a culture-wide, pervasive indoctrination children are receiving that, in extreme forms at least, is resulting in this strange imbalance —more boys having problems in elementary school years, more girls in high school and adult years." At this point I went back to my graduate school readings on sex-role socialization, looked at the patterns that had been reported there, and found two characteristics that have been widely reported. The characteristics of male and female sex roles include aggressive behavior on the male side and dependent behavior— dependency and passivity—on the female.

It seemed clear to me that if one trained children to an extreme degree to be either aggressive or passive and dependent, they were likely to have problems. But how does this come about? If something about boys' socialization is teaching them to be aggressive, they're going to have problems in elementary schools. If something about girls' socialization is teaching them to be dependent, they're not going to have such noticeable problems in elementary school, but they are going to have problems when they become adolescents, and are suddenly expected to be independent and to begin to function as adults. When they've been socialized as youngsters to be dependent on others, this could lead to tremendous conflicts. In fact, there is a good deal of literature relating dependent personality characteristics to all kinds of psychological problems, especially fears, anxiety-related problems, and depression.

Aggressive Behaviors

I decided to go and look in the preschool *before* children enter public schools and the behavior problems reported for boys begin to result in psychological referrals. In this first study, we observed systematically in 15 different classrooms at four schools. Over the entire semester this involved over 60 hours of observation time that included children and teachers from a variety of socio-economic backgrounds. (A detailed description of the methods used in this study may be found in Serbin, O'Leary, Kento, Fonick, 1973.) The project focused on the children's behavior and also on the teachers' reactions to what the children did. Were there different contingencies in effect for boys and girls, contingencies that might shape sex differences in behavior, if they weren't there already? And if sex differences *were* there already, were the teachers reacting differently in ways that would maintain these differences or strengthen them?

The first thing we examined was teachers' responses to disruptive classroom behavior, including their responses to aggression, to children who ignored their directions, and to children engaged in deliberate destruction of materials. How did the teachers react? The results we obtained were very similar for all three forms of disruptive classroom behavior. I'll illustrate what we found with a story, one I find especially dramatic because it involved not only the teachers but also the other children in the room.

One morning we were observing a class of four-and-a-half-year-olds during free play. We saw a group of little boys playing with tinker toy materials. One boy reached for another child's piece of tinker toy and tried to snatch it away from him. The second child hung onto the tinker toy and resisted. The first child lifted his hand, obviously ready to strike. Instantly there was a chorus in that room: "Mrs. Jones, John's hitting." There was John with his hand up in the air, and all the other children were shouting, "John's hitting him."

Mrs. Jones said, "John, I told you. We don't hit in here. What is going on over here, boys?" She walked over to them and said, "What was it? Oh, Billy wouldn't share the tinker toy. Well, okay, Billy, you know you have to share with John." The whole class was standing there watching this. The incident had now become the central focus of the classroom. "John, we don't hit when we want something. You'll have to wait your turn. I'm sure Billy is going to share with you, aren't you, Billy?"

We recorded this incident. The observers put down "John, aggression." One tally mark in the aggression column. "Teacher, loud reprimand." (Loud reprimand was defined as a comment the rest of the children could hear.)

A little bit later in the same classroom, three little girls were playing in the kitchen corner. One little girl tried to take away a set of dishes that another girl was playing with. She snatched for them. The second little girl pulled away her dishes. The first little girl raised her hand, and this time actually followed through with a slap. The second little girl looked at her, pulled the dishes farther away, and moved two steps down the counter. At least two other children saw this. Nobody said anything. The teacher didn't say anything.

After our observations in all 15 rooms, it became clear that there was a relatively low probability that anybody would react when a girl hit. Seventy-five percent of the time that boys struck someone else, or even moved their hand in that direction, teachers would intervene, most of the time with a "loud" reprimand that everyone in the room could hear. Only 25 percent of the time that girls were aggressive did teachers say anything and most often gave a "soft" reprimand, audible only to the girl herself, when they responded at all.

Why do teachers react differently to boys' and girls' aggression? Obviously, teachers may be responding to sex differences in children's behavior. If you ask teachers about these patterns, they'll say, "Boys hit more often. We're much more sensitized to it. Also they hit harder. They're bigger. We just notice it a lot more, and we're more worried about it, because we know that they have a problem in this area. So we intervene." But what is the result of this type of intervention?

John, in that instance, learned that he can 1) get a tremendous amount of attention and 2) eventually get to share that tinker toy by hitting another child. At the least, he knows he'll get a squeal from the victim. If you're angry and frustrated, that could be reinforcing right by itself, to hear somebody else get upset also. For girls, there's no response. It just doesn't work for a girl to try to hit somebody. At least, it doesn't work very often. Teachers quite inadvertently seem to be strengthening the pattern they're trying to discourage in boys, while teaching girls that physical aggression is not effective.

It should be obvious at this point that different treatment of boys and girls hurts boys as much as it hurts girls. I think that this is often underestimated in talks about sexism in the classroom and sex-role stereotyping.

Dependent Behaviors

Let me turn now to girls, because I think disruptive behavior and other school-related problems more typical of boys have been studied a great deal. Dependent behavior as a problem area is usually ignored, because a quiet child does not receive the same kind of attention from a teacher as a disruptive child. A girl who is socialized to be passive and dependent may be perceived as a good student, since she is quiet, compliant, docile, and so forth. I do not think these children have received the attention that they deserve, because a child who is socialized in this mode may well have trouble later on when conflicts resulting in emotional problems emerge in adolescence and adulthood.

The antecedents of these problems seem to develop during the preschool period when patterns of dependency and passivity begin to develop. In our study we examined teachers' reactions to dependent behaviors. We observed how teachers interacted with children who were immediately proximal to them versus a little farther away (the other side of the table or elsewhere within eye and ear contact). Here we found a very subtle and interesting pattern. Little boys received approximately constant levels of teacher attention, praise, comments, and instruction, regardless of whether they were beside the teacher or farther away (these were all unsolicited comments). In other words, teachers would notice what a boy was doing, find it interesting, and interact with him. With girls, there was differential attention paid according to how close they were to the teacher. Girls were learning, "I can stay near the teacher and I'll get attention. If I go farther away, I'm going to be ignored." To the boys, no such message came across since teachers noticed them and talked to them from a distance as well as when they were playing immediately beside them.

Why do teachers do this? Is this pattern deliberate? I don't think so. I don't think they're deliberately teaching little girls to "hang around." In fact, our teachers complained about it saying, "I don't like it. They're just not as interesting as the boys. They hang around. They don't get into their own things. They don't explore." We sat down with these teachers and showed them the observation records. They were quite honestly not aware of their own reactions. They did not see that they were socializing the very dependent behaviors in girls that they found so irritating and uninteresting. Why did they respond differently? Boys' behavior may be more salient. The teachers argued that it was, that it was more noticeable, that boys did things in a "bigger way." Boys have more trouble doing things. They aren't as well coordinated. The girls could be trusted to "pick things up on their own." However, the effect of reacting in this "natural" way to differences in boys' and girls' behavior may be to exaggerate, reinforce, encourage, or maintain whatever sex differences in independence, motor coordination, and learning abilities are present when children walked into the room.

In this study, we also looked at attention given to the children when they were behaving appropriately. They were not clinging nor hitting; they were just doing what they were supposed to do during free play. Many earlier studies on this topic are difficult to interpret because they don't take into account what the children may have done that elicited differential responses from teachers. For example, if boys raise their hands or call out more than girls, obviously they're going to get more attention.

In our study we observed differences in the children's behavior and tried to allow for them. Given that a child was playing or working appropriately, what was the probability the teacher would become involved? We found this pattern: more interaction with the boys, more praise, and, one of our most interesting findings, a difference in the kinds of instruction given to boys and girls. Boys received more detailed step-by-step instruction in how to solve a problem or how to do something for themselves. Eight times as much instruction was given boys as to girls. Eight times! When we asked teachers about it, they replied, "Boys need that kind of instruction much more than girls do. Girls pick stuff up on their own." Perhaps the teachers are right. I'm not willing to

Teachers, Peers, and Play Preferences • 85

abandon the hypothesis that girls at that age may be better socialized and better coordinated. Maybe they *can* use scissors without being taught how to use it before boys can. But what is the effect of boys receiving that much more step-by-step instruction, that much detailed analysis, that much modeling? What is the effect on children's learning how to do things for themselves and learning how to analyze a problem?

Teachers, of course, are not the sole or primary enforcers of sex-role patterns. Parents, peers, and media are all major contributors. Nevertheless, these teachers were reinforcing patterns of sex-role learning that are pervasive in American society.

What happens when these patterns are shifted around? We tried to reverse some of the reinforcement patterns for dependency we had observed (Serbin, Connor and Citron, in press) and set up controlled designs to evaluate the effectiveness of reversing these patterns. We found that when teachers did not reinforce proximity seeking by little girls and attended to the children essentially at a constant level, regardless of proximity, initially there was an increase in clinging. But this dropped off within a few minutes. We found that proximity seeking, hanging around the teacher, by both girls and boys reduced sharply. Not only did girls work at greater distances from the teacher, but they also increased their exploration of the room and played with more toys. We also found an increase in task persistence. The kids worked for longer periods of time on their own without trying to involve the teacher in their projects. These were very encouraging results, and really all it took was a teacher being aware and making sure that the children received attention when they were working a little bit farther away, rather than primarily when they were right beside her.

Sex Typing and Cognitive Development

We also focused on the development of cognitive and learning skills that may be hindered by the sex typing process. One of the primary goals of a nursery school is to encourage children to explore new roles. Children are at nursery school to learn to do new things, to be exposed to new experiences, to learn to interact with people they haven't met before, people from other groups and other backgrounds, and to explore, trying out new things, new toys, new behaviors, and new activities. Schools also function to help children develop their individual abilities to the greatest possible extent, to provide opportunities for them to grow in new directions where they haven't yet had the impulse or opportunity to explore.

It is widely believed that the activities in which children engage in preschool will have an impact on the roles they will practice and the skills they will develop. Blocks are in the room for a very specific purpose. Playing with blocks helps eye-hand coordination and teaches children to build in three dimensions. Similarly, dolls are in the classroom for a specific reason also—practicing nurturant roles. However, as anyone who has observed a preschool knows, toys that children actually play with in the classroom are very definitely affected by sex-role stereotypes.

Children do not come in and randomly play with every toy in the room. By the time children walk into the nursery school classroom, sex preferences for specific toys and activities are already present. As a result of this, children do not take the opportunity to explore every toy in the room but rather play with certain toys and develop certain skills according to the sex-typed labels they have learned.

As early as age four, there is a definite relationship between conformity to "masculine" and "feminine" activity preferences and specific patterns for cognitive development. For example, visual-spatial problem solving ability is believed to be an important factor in mathematics and science achievement, and sex differences in both these areas appear later on in the school years. We found that preschool children who play primarily with "boys' toys" such as blocks, trucks, and climbing apparatus showed stronger visual-spatial problem solving abilities than children who play primarily with "girls' toys" including dolls, housekeeping materials, and fine motor activities (Connor and Serbin, in press). Sex differences in visual-spatial ability are not yet present during the preschool period, but these data suggest that sex-typed activity patterns may contribute to later sex differences in problem solving ability and achievement.

Sex Typing of Play Activities

In one study we asked teachers in nine classrooms to introduce three new toys to their classes. A fishing set had been labeled "masculine" by adult and child raters, sewing cards as "feminine," and a third, a counting puzzle game, was rated non-sex-typed. We asked teachers to show each toy to their class and to call on several children to help demonstrate its use to the other children. The teachers responded to the sex typing of the toys, introducing the fishing set with stories of "going fishing with daddy" and the sewing cards "like when mommy sews on a button." In addition, the teachers called on many more boys than girls to demonstrate the fishing set to the class, and, when introducing the sewing cards, also reacted in terms of the sex stereotypes. Only when introducing the non-sex-typed toy did the teachers call on boys and girls indiscriminately.

The effects of sex-typed introductions and use of male versus female models to demonstrate specific toys has been shown in many laboratory studies (Liebert, McCall and Hanratty, 1971; Montemeyor, 1974). Children readily learned whether a toy is sex "appropriate" or "inappropriate" from such introductions. The fact that nursery school teachers introduce activities in this manner suggests that they are providing children with sex-typed labels for these activities. Children are learning that the teacher expects either boys or girls to play with a particular toy.

Another observational study focused on a more subtle pattern that tended to prevent exploration of new toys. Beverly Fagot and Gerald Patterson (1969) found that teachers interacted with children of both sexes primarily when activities were female-preferred. In other words, their time with boys and girls was spent in the activities girls like, so that their interactions with boys were primarily in female sex-typed activities. Now this seemed puzzling. If teachers are reinforcing boys by engaging in girls' activities (which is one way of interpreting this finding), why don't boys start to play with these toys? Doesn't this argue that reinforcement doesn't have much of an impact?

Here's a different interpretation of this data. . . . Teachers, perhaps because they are socialized as females (and these were female teachers), have certain interests in a classroom. They're also trained to focus on certain things. Traditionally teachers have been trained to encourage fine motor tasks. In a free play situation teachers will spend a good deal of their time sitting at a table interacting with the kids who are making things: craft activities, drawing, and so forth. How much time do preschool teachers spend with the trucks and blocks? Relatively little.

Since teachers seem to focus on certain activities as a result of their own interest and training, the question asked in this particular study was, "Is it possible that girls do not explore certain areas because they have been socialized to follow the teacher around?" I described above how we observed teachers reinforcing proximity seeking by little girls. Is it possible that the reason girls don't get into the blocks and the trucks is because the teacher doesn't get into the blocks and the trucks either? To find out, we did a very simple study: we asked a teacher to simply place herself in the block area for a little while. This is what happened (Serbin, Connor and Citron, 1977).

First the little boys were in the block area. When the teacher joined them, they continued with what they were doing. A little girl very shortly wandered by and looked around. She was holding a doll. This happened to be a little girl we had never observed in the block area before. She was a "follower," one of the proximity seekers. She stood there for a little while and then picked up a block and began to play. Gradually other little girls drifted in. After ten minutes that whole block corner was occupied by boys and girls; half the children had never been in that area before.

We also asked the teacher to do the same thing with dolls, with the same effect. This time little boys who had not played with dolls before entered the doll corner. Again their hesitancy was interesting. They hung around for a while and looked. It took them about five minutes to really become involved in playing with the dolls. No "coercion" was involved at all. The teacher never said, "Bobby, why don't you come over here?" She just sat there. It was quite dramatic.

Now the interesting thing to us was that both sexes responded; both girls and boys ventured into the others' sex "territory." But perhaps more interesting from a theoretical perspective was that girls responded about twice as much as boys did. In other words, these results provided strong support for the idea that girls' interests are being developed by the fact that teachers spend their time in certain areas. Girls are more likely to follow their teachers no matter where they are in the classroom.

We have since repeated this study with both male and female teachers (the first study involved only a female teacher) and found that girls again tended to follow teachers wherever they went. Boys, however, were particularly responsive to modeling of traditionally masculine activities by the male teachers. For example, a male teacher in the block area was a much more powerful model for boys than the same male teacher in the doll or kitchen area, or than a female teacher in either type of activity. For this reason, I believe it is especially important for male teachers to be aware of where they spend their time in the classroom. If they stay in the vicinity of traditionally masculine activities, this will effectively keep the boys in these areas also.

Our conclusion from these studies is that teacher presence and modeling is an extremely powerful factor in determining children's activites. If female teachers stay in the "feminine" areas, while male teachers focus on "masculine" activities, their classrooms are likely to reflect their own (probably sex-typed) developmental and educational histories. However, we have found that when teachers are made aware of these patterns, they are willing and able to diversify.

Peers and Play Preferences

Peers, of course, also influence sex typing in classrooms. Children seem to conform not only to their perceptions of teachers' expectations but to peer expectations as well. To demonstrate the power of this effect, we recently did a study in which children were taken individually to a playroom containing a variety of male and female stereotyped toys (Serbin, Connor, Burchardt, and Citron, 1977).

Initially the children were very stereotyped in their toy selection choices. But when we left them for a little while, they started to explore. A boy would play with the dishes and the doll; a girl would throw airplanes around the room. However, this relaxation of stereotypes didn't happen when another child was present in the room, and it especially didn't happen when the child was of the opposite sex. A little boy sitting coloring a picture at a desk in the room was enough to keep little girls with their dishes and dolls. We found the same effect in reverse for boys. A little girl coloring a picture in the room kept them with their trucks and planes. We concluded that just the presence of a peer, especially an opposite sex peer, is likely to make a child conform to sex-role stereotypes. In a classroom, it is easy to see that children may avoid certain toys and play areas they have learned are sex-role inappropriate if other children, especially of the opposite sex, are nearby.

Rates of cooperative play between boys and girls are typically much lower than between same sex children. This may also keep children from exploring particular toys. In other words, if boys and girls primarily play separately rather than together, it is likely that boys will continue playing primarily with "boys' toys" and the girls with "girls' toys."

Fortunately, we found that this pattern is not difficult to reverse (Serbin, Tonick, and Sternglanz, 1977). When teachers indicate that they expect and approve of cross-sex, cooperative play, by simply commenting on it when it occurs, boys and girls do begin to play more with each other. Comments such as, "John and Cathy are building a very high tower with the blocks" effectively convey to children that playing with someone of the opposite sex is not disapproved of (a message they are likely to have received pervasively from sex-stereotyping indoctrination outside the classroom).

Freeing Children from Sex-role Stereotypes

Children come into a preschool classroom heavily "programmed." They have already learned that different characteristics, activities, and behaviors are expected of males and females. They will conform to these sex roles in the classroom unless the teacher makes an active effort to communicate different expectations and values. If children are to be freed from stereotyping, they must be treated as individuals, rather than as members of a classified group. Teachers will have to make special efforts to introduce all toys to all the children. They will have to encourage children to take turns at all the activities, to explore new activities, and to engage in cooperative play with both boys and girls. We've shown that these things can be done effectively, but teachers will have to offset powerful home, peer, and media influences. It's certainly a long-term project—you can't expect it to happen in a morning or even in two weeks.

The process of freeing children from stereotypes will have to counter children's own tendencies to stereotype. For example, one day the children in our nursery school were running around the track at our university. They love to do this and to "time" themselves, to see how fast they are. After all the children had run and had been timed, Michele was acclaimed the fastest in the class, and all the children took a final sprint around the track with their teacher. While they were running, they were passed by a female student who was running on the track. One of the boys looked up at the teacher with a very puzzled look on his face. He said, "What's she doing here? Girls can't run!" Chucky was running next to his teacher, who was also running and was a female, and Chucky had just acknowledged that the fastest child in his class, Michele, was a girl.

Children do seem to filter out information that runs counter to their expectations or to their stereotypes. To change these, children will have to be taught that specific behaviors, specific roles, and specific interests are not part of "being a boy" or "being a girl." Being a girl does not mean that one has to be passive and not able to run very fast. Children have to learn, have to be taught, that specific activities and specific roles are not exclusively assigned to one sex or the other.

Conclusion

To summarize the findings I've reported, we discovered that teachers reinforce sex-role stereotypes in many subtle ways of which they are frequently not aware. We also found, however, that teachers can reverse these patterns effectively when they become aware of them. We demonstrated that increased independence, cooperative play between boys and girls, and exploration of all classroom activities by children of both sexes can be accomplished, if a teacher wishes to do so.

Will this mean a great deal of artificial programming or coercion? I don't think so. After all, teachers, like the rest of society, are already heavily "programmed" to train and enforce traditional sex roles, which place arbitrary limits on the direction and extent of each child's individual development. Actually, I see the role of the preschool teacher as a powerful force to combat some of the pervasive stereotyping that children receive during the preschool period. As psychologists and educators have long been aware, this is the period when sex roles are learned. Learning during the preschool period may also, thus, be a key to introducing children to more flexible, rather than sex-role determined, patterns of behavior. The preschool period may, in fact, be a critical time for prevention of the cognitive and emotional handicaps that can result from conformity to rigid sex roles. From our data, it is clear that teachers will have to do more than "not enforce" traditional sex-role stereotypes in their classrooms if they wish children to be free to develop as individuals. They will have to play a most active part in the process.

The methods I've described involve little that could be labeled "coercive" or "manipulative." Teachers simply introduced toys to *all* the children, or "modeled" a greater variety of activities, or stopped responding differentially to passivity and aggression by boys and girls. These methods do, however, require an active awareness and involvement. Teachers will have to be loving enough and concerned enough to analyze their own behavior and, if necessary, make some changes.

RELEVANT RESEARCH REPORTS

Connor, J.M., and Serbin. L.A. "Behaviorally-Based Masculine and Feminine Activity Preference Scales for Preschoolers: Correlates With Other Classroom Behaviors and Cognitive Tests," *Child Development*, in press.

Fagot, B.I., and Patterson, G.R. An *in Vivo* Analysis of Reinforcing Contingencies for Sex-role Behaviors in the Preschool Child. *Developmental Psychology*, Vol. 1, 1969, pp. 563-568.

Liebert, R.M., Call, R.B., and Hanratty, M.A. "Effects of Sex-typed Information on Children's Log Preference." *Journal of Genetic Psychology*, 1971, pp. 119, 133-136.

Montemayor, R. "Children's Performance in a Game and Their Attraction to It as a Function of Sex-typed Labels. *Child Development*, Vol. 45, 1974, pp. 152-156.

Serbin, L.A., Connor, J.M., Burchardt, C., and Citron, C.C. Effects of Peer Presence on Sex-Typing of Children's Toy Choices. Paper presented to the Society for Research and Child Development, New Orleans, La., March, 1977.

Serbin, L.A., Connor, J.M., Burchardt, C., Sex-Stereotyped Play Behavior in the Preschool Classroom: Effects of Teacher Presence and Modeling. Paper presented to Society for Research and Child Development, New Orleans, La., March, 1977

———. Environmental Control of Independent and Dependent Behaviors in Preschool Girls and Boys: A Model for Early Independence Training. *Sex Roles*, in press.

Serbin, L.A. and O'Leary, K.D. "How Nursery Schools Teach Girls to Shut Up." *Psychology Today*, December 1975.

———. Kent, R.N., and Tonick, I.J. "A Comparison of Teacher Response to the Preacademic and Problem Behavior of Boys and Girls. *Child Development*, Vol. 44, 1973, pp. 796-804.

Serbin, L.A., Tonick, I.J., and Sternglanz, S.H. "Shaping Cooperative Cross-Sex Play," *Child Development*, in press.

7

The Development of Psychological Androgyny: Early Childhood Socialization

DR. JOAN P. BEAN

**Dean and Professor of Psychology
Wheaton College**

FEW aspects of human development have so preoccupied researchers in the last decade as socialization—the process of instilling in children social values and sex roles. Any attempt to synthesize the data becomes a Herculean effort, not only because of the sheer volume of research but also because of contemporary changes in perspective and sex-role behavior. No sooner is one socialization variable pinned down—for example, the achievement motive—than it slips away in qualifications reflecting individual and cultural changes. The entire research enterprise seems to suffer from something like a "cultural lag."

One can examine sex-typed behavior as the status quo—this research represents the "cultural lag"—and/or describe sex-role change in a social and cultural context. My concern is to show how socio-cultural factors shape sex-role identification and to demonstrate the socio-cultural factors that lead to androgyny. What are the major influences? Who are the socializing agents? How do they influence young children? I will briefly examine the major themes of the psychoanalytic, the social learning, and cognitive developmental theories.

Three Theories of Sex-Role Development

The psychoanalytic model, first introduced by Freud, assumes the overriding significance of biology and early experience in sex-role development. The theory predicts a lifelong stability of masculine qualities for males and feminine qualities for females, ignoring the influences of the cultural environment. The child is seen as the passive recipient of an inevitable program of complexes, which include envy of body parts and the desire to avoid punishment for "taboo" feelings. Within this framework, sex-role change is not possible; individuals have, in fact, little control over life events. Compounding this determinism, the psychoanalytic theory predicts adult personal adjustment on a rigid adherence to the program of psychosexual development. The validity of Freud's psychoanalytic socialization model has been challenged by psychotherapists and clients.

The second model, social learning theory, emerged from the Skinnerian experimental tradition. Using the basic tenets of learning theory —stimulus, response, and reinforcement—the social learning position predicts acquisition of sex-role behavior that proceeds in the same way other behaviors are learned—that is, by systematic reinforcement from the environment. Although those espousing this position have elaborated the behaviorist theory by including "imitation" and "modeling" of adults, a child is still seen as an "empty organism" passively receiving rewards and punishments for appropriate and inappropriate sex-role behavior.

The major focus here is primarily on events in the environment that "shape" a child's sex-role behavior. Alternative sex roles, according to the behaviorist model, are possible only if the external reinforcements for specific behaviors change. From this position, little can be said about internal individual motivation. The major problems with this socialization theory are: 1) most of the empirical work has been carried out within the confines of the experimental laboratory; 2) to date, no one has demonstrated the specific antecedents of differential sex-role learning; and 3) the evidence for parental reinforcement of sex-appropriate and -inappropriate behavior is weak.

Cognitive developmental theory, in contrast with the social learning explanation of socialization, suggests a more active role for the child. Lawrence Kohlberg, the major proponent of the theory, uses Piaget's cognitive stage framework to explain sex-role learning as a function of a child's interaction with his or her environment. The level of cognitive growth constrains the kind and amount of information a child assimilates and accommodates. Sex becomes one of many categories around which a child can structure the environment. This step is followed, according to Kohlberg, by the valuing of same-sex behaviors and attitudes and the devaluing of opposite-sex behaviors and attitudes. At this point, females and males imitate same-sex models, thus learning the appropriate sex role behaviors. Kohlberg applies his formulation mostly to male sex-role development, leaving the socialization process for females rather undeveloped. Although the model attempts to encompass the child and the socio-cultural environment, the child's internal cognitive structure is the major focus.

Cognitive developmental theory, like psychoanalytic and social learning theories, halts at the status quo once sex typing is explained. The underlying norm permeating the theoretical explanations of sex-role socialization is that of the WASP male, and the underlying assumption—by now familiar—is that the more sex typing there is, the better the adjustment. Until recently, few researchers have challenged the socio-cultural stereotypes. What would happen if the cultural norms and sex stereotypes were eliminated? What would serve as the plan for female and male socialization? What human qualities might develop as the masculine and feminine roles merge and blend?

Theory of Psychological Androgyny

The new alternative theory I am presenting is one of psychological androgyny. Although the theory is *not* well developed—I cannot lay out the stages a child might go through to emerge as androgynous—I can share the "promise" of androgyny. Most of the ground work and foundation has been laid by Sandra Bem, a psychologist from Stanford University—an important foremother.

When I use the concept psychological androgyny, I mean flexibility of sex role. I am not referring to individuals with male and female sex organs, but to people who are capable of behaving in integrative feminine *and* masculine ways, who are assertive and yielding, independent and dependent, expressive and instrumental. Androgynous people not only survive but thrive in our changing society. I do not mean a union of extreme masculine and extreme feminine qualities; a dependent passive-aggressive person is not androgynous. Androgyny includes masculine and feminine traits but moves beyond these to a third integrated dimension that is influenced by individual differences across situations and over a lifetime. It is the flexibility and union of positively valued traits that is critical for the concept.

One of the problems with the model of psychological androgyny is that it assumes a separate content for masculinity and femininity. Moving beyond these distinctions to a third dimension is central to the formulation. Transcending sex roles is being androgynous. Theoretically, androgynous behavior differs from behavior that alternates between being masculine and being feminine; it is the integration of these that is crucial.

The critical socializers in early childhood are parents and teachers. From birth, when the physician announces "It's a girl" or "It's a boy," parents differentially perceive their infant daughters and sons. Parents see daughters as "more delicate, weaker, and little" and their sons as "firmer, large featured, more alert, sturdier, and hardier." The sex-typed parental responses occur in spite of data confirming *no* sex differences in physical and health characteristics. Fathers do more extreme stereotyping of both infant daughters and sons. However, as I know from my own experience, hospitals are reluctant to allow fathers "handling" privileges, thus excluding fathers from the early interaction and nurturance of infants. If fathers were more involved in infant care, would they perceive more similarities between their infant sons and daughters? Perhaps including fathers directly in child-rearing would change their perceptions and would lead to less stereotyped expectations. Future parents, then, might be more responsive to the existence of sex similarities—androgyny—than the differences dictated by cultural sex roles.

In a field study across three cultures (American, Western European, and African) researchers (Whiting and Edwards, 1973) found young children exhibit a complex set of stereotypes at play and at work. Three- to eleven-year-old males and females have different styles of dominance and dependence. These styles emerge from different socialization pressures and task assignments within the culture. Where dependency might be defined as seeking attention, seven-to-eleven year-old males are more dependent than their female peers. Young girls are more dependent than boys only when dependency is defined as seeking help and physical contact. The locale of socialization may be important; girls are kept closer to home performing chores that require compliance and nurturance when interacting with adults and infants, while boys are allowed a wider range of distance, away from the domestic demands of adults and infants.

There are individual expressions of personality and different ages at which the culture presses for a specific trait. Certain behaviors decrease with age; as children mature, they need less support from older peers and adults. Boys' attention-seeking behavior seems a direct reflection of social pressures that do not exist at an earlier age. What would happen if the work assignments of males and females were reversed? In cultures where boys engage in child care and domestic chores, fewer sex differences were found; boys more frequently engage in helping and cooperative group behavior. Domestic tasks may foster androgynous behavior for boys; girls working in fields may develop androgynous behavior. I would suggest that cross-sex classroom tasks may foster androgynous behavior. Why have we been so persistent in work assignments in technological societies?

In a study of the middle-class subculture of schools and homes, Patricia Minuchin (1965) contrasted the sex-role attitudes and sex-typing of nine-year-olds in "modern" and "traditional" schools. The modern viewpoint is operationally defined as one "fostering the individual development of the child." Parental standards reflect a child's talents and motivation; school standards reflect the value of exploration, mastery, and flexibility. Sex roles in this pattern were open. I think these values would facilitate androgyny because they focus on intellectual and personal diversity, not conformity.

The traditional viewpoint was more authoritarian; parents stressed adherence to socially approved rules and methods. The schools fostered competitive achievement based on a body of established knowledge. Sex roles were seen as fixed, and appropriate sex-role behavior was rewarded. The results suggest an interesting pattern of social change. Girls from modern middle-class families and schools expressed less sex-typing and more role openness than any other group. This *limited* white middle-class sample suggests a clear move away from traditional orientations toward less specific sex-role standards.

These data support the hypothesis that children—especially girls—are being affected by the shift to flexible open roles. Children from lower-middle-class families, however, and more traditional schools were more socialized toward fixed sex-role standards. Boys expressed more aggressive fantasy; girls expressed more domestic fantasy. The implications of this study are somewhat restricted; we do not know what factors provoked less sex-typing nor what specific behaviors of teachers and parents influenced the development of more flexible sex roles. Does social class alone predict more or less role flexibility? It seems equally possible that children of employed working-class mothers might also be less sex-typed. Future research might include a broader socio-economic range along with more specific behaviors.

Areas for Future Research

So far research has focused on the major socializing agents—parents, cultures, and the schools. Each study includes some aspect of the learning environment—the hospital, the socio-cultural context, the school. Unlike much published research, observations have been made in naturalistic, real-life settings. The set of studies I've reviewed has been selected to demonstrate the constraints of a social context.

Future research might examine the parental expectations of those choosing to have infants delivered at home. Would their attitudes be the same as parents selecting a hospital setting? Are children who participate in cross-sex work assignments less sex-typed than those performing sex-typed chores? In the classroom, which factors influence androgynous behavior, curriculum, school values, and interactions between children and teacher? Are girls who take math and science courses androgynous? Are boys who enroll in literature and art courses androgynous?

Moving back to the family, androgynous adults grow up in families where mothers *and* fathers did not typify cultural sex-role stereotypes. However, even in families with low sex-typed models and egalitarian relationships between parents, males fare better than females. This generalization from the Berkeley Growth Study suggests that androgynous women a generation ago were rare people. Perhaps, with the sex-role changes we are experiencing, females will receive more support and encouragement.

How can one encourage the flexibility of sex role I call androgyny? I have no curriculum to share—the behavioral expression of attitudes and values is the hidden non-sexist curriculum. Teachers' ability to transcend the stereotypes will be critical to a generation of children.

REFERENCES

Minuchin, Patricia. "Sex Role Concepts and Sex Typing in Childhood as a Function of School and Home Environments," *Child Development*, Vol. 36, 1965, pp. 133-148.

Whiting, Beatrice, and Edwards, Carolyn Pope. "A Cross-Cultural Analysis of Sex Differences in the Behavior of Children Age Three to Eleven," *Journal of Social Psychology*, Vol. 91, 1973, pp. 171-188.

8

Sex Differences in The Use of Outdoor Space

DR. ROGER HART

Research Associate
Department of Environmental Psychology
City University of New York, Graduate
Division

W HILE conducting observations of children's exploration, knowledge of, and feelings for the environment in a small New England town, I was initially shocked to find the extent to which the physical environment is essentially boys' domain (Hart, 1977). A little simple retrospection of my own childhood and that of my peers, however, supported my observations. The surprising part was that the behavorial sciences had barely noted this phenomenon. Until recently, studies of child development commonly failed to look at sex differences at all, but recently researchers have come to realize that boys and girls may be differentially treated by adults in many ways according to their sex, even before children are of an age to know themselves that they are male or female.

Exploring Environments

The aspect of behavior that first led me to look closely at the different behavior of boys and girls, in what was primarily a developmental study, were clear differences in the parentally defined spatial range restrictions of children over six years of age. This by itself is an interesting observation for there is no biological basis for different treatment. Findings of studies on the activity levels of boys and girls are not very consistent, but, overall, the summary of evidence suggests no sex differences during the first year of life (Maccoby and Jacklin, 1974).

The question is, to what extent do parents' attitudes lead them to make different environmental experiences available to girls and boys through the encouragement or restriction of certain types of activities?

Research on sex-role socialization is very difficult to conduct because the process of learning is interactive from the very beginning of a child's life. It is hard to know whether or to what degree a mother responds to inherent differences in an infant's behavior or whether all of the differences in treatment may be explained by her different attitude toward rearing girls versus boys.

Lewis (1972) has found that from birth to six months of age boys were more likely to experience touching, holding, kissing, and rocking from the mother than were girls, but that after this time the pattern was reversed. At two years, he found boys more willing to venture farther away from the mother, and he concluded that during the first two years of life, the socialization taking place weans boys away from maintaining physical contact with others to a much greater extent than for girls.

In my study I asked each child in the town to describe "the area you are allowed to play in outside your house by yourself, without asking special permission from your parents." The children found it easy to describe this area using environmental details and, because of my familiarity with the area, I was able to draw the boundary lines on a large-scale aerial photograph. Follow-up interviews with the parents of six families representing sixteen children confirmed the accuracy of these descriptions. It was not possible to make statistical comparisons by annual age groups as the sample was too small for some ages, but it was possible to group the data and consider the five- to eight-year-olds and the nine- to twelve-year-olds. In both age groups the boys' range is larger than the girls' but most markedly so in the older age group. By the age of ten years, the boys' ranges increased dramatically and restrictions were largely removed.

Similar findings have been made by Margaret Tindal (1971) with second- and fourth-grade children in both urban and suburban environments in Maryland, for Puerto Rican children (Landy, 1957), and with Bantu-speaking children in Kenya (Munroe and Munroe, 1971; Nerlove, Munroe, and Munroe, 1971). However, a need for further study remains. There is certainly sufficient evidence to question the belief in Maccoby and Jacklin's otherwise excellent review that no sex differences exist in independence granting. Maccoby and Jacklin were led to their conclusion by the fact that most of the studies reviewed were of four- to five-year-old children; this is easily the most studied group in child psychology, largely because it is the most accessible population for study! But the studies cited above suggest a gradual increase in boy-girl differences with age. Clearly boys are being given more freedom than girls.

Few conditions for these differences in behavior have been offered. Maccoby and Jacklin suggest that parents have a greater fear of molestation of girls and that this is an anticipation of further chaperonage in adolescence. My informal observations on this question in the New England town were that while this may have been in the minds of some parents, the greater restraint of girls was related to a whole complex of attitudes to boys versus girls. The most striking feature of my interviews with the children about parental range restrictions, and the one that led me to first notice the many sex differences in my data, was the ambiguous response I received from the boys as opposed to the girls.

Boys would describe one boundary and then give the name of another place beyond the boundary. On further questioning, it would commonly be revealed that the rules, usually made by both parents, were, in fact, administered by the mother only and that she often turned a "blind eye" where her boy broke the boundary: "Well, she knows that I go, but I'm not supposed to." Such comments as this were most frequently made by the older boys in the town. Again from casual observations, I noted that should a boy get into trouble outside of the formally agreed upon range, such as falling into the river, he would be punished. Implicit in this special treatment given to boys by their mothers seems to be the attitude that "boys will be boys," meaning that they are expected to explore more, engage in more rough play, be more physically active, and even get into more trouble, but that they must expect punishment equal to, or maybe even greater than, that given to girls. Such are their attitudes toward the making of a man.

Building Environments

I also observed that boys modify the landscape more frequently and more effectively than girls. For example, in creating settings for their play, boys build physical structures much more frequently than girls. Girls also have houses, forts, and so on, but they physically manipulate the environment less. More often they modify the spaces in their imagination, so that bushes become walls, lateral branches of trees become shelves, and rocks are used as seats. Such imaginative creation of space also occurs with boys' places, but commonly, after about seven years of age, boys build forts and other structures with walls, windows, seats, and even roofs. When girls do build such places, rarely do they create walls, even though considerable effort may go towards the detailed elaboration of the interior with drapes, bottles, pots, and pans. None of the structures built entirely by girls had fixed walls or roofs.

Also, boys made many more models in the dirt, manipulated streams with dams and channels, made and managed gardens, built sled runs and jumps, and in general made their mark on the landscape more than girls. On the few occasions when I did observe girls creating models in the dirt, alone or with other girls, they built houses and rooms and decorated the interiors and pathways, while boys built cities, highways, airports, and race tracks. When girls were found engaged in these latter activities, it was in play with boys. [1]

Generally building was organized and engineered by older boys, while girls and younger boys assisted with water carrying. Girls would frequently build subsidiary systems around the edges, an activity that disturbed the boys. On a particular day of filming, the girls arrived early and began very competent dam building. When the boys arrived, they moved in with critical comments and much arguing to take over the central dam activity. This was a particularly clear example of how girls are constrained to conform to sex-role stereotypes by male peers as well as by adults. The principal of the school had on a number of occasions needed to affirm the girls' right to build outdoors over parental discomfort with the girls getting their clothes dirty.

Based on my observations I suggest that environmental education and recreation programs using the outdoor environment of the school should generally encourage girls to feel free to take an active role in exploring and manipulating the physical environment. This would include, for example, girls taking leading roles in the design and execution of child-lead field trips and in designing and building places in the school and schoolgrounds. Not getting dirty and wearing certain types of clothing may be relevant immediate explanation factors but there is a more important and more embracing explanation: *girls have come to believe that they are less able to build things.*

At early ages dirt building was the most common activity for all, but particularly for boys. Furthermore, boys generally built roads systems and towns, and girls built interior spaces. On one occasion, while interviewing all the children in the school about their "favorite places," I was pleasantly surprised to find a fourth-grade girl describing a "giant city" that had been built in the back of her house. In pursuing this interesting discussion, however, my pleasure was quickly subdued as the girl explained the "city" was built by an older boy and that she could not possibly have built anything like this by herself because she was a girl and "only boys know how to build things." She described how, because of this, she and her younger sister only helped make the roads and cleaned things up.

Why should an extremely confident and competent girl, rated at the top of her grade in school, speak this way? I believe the answer lies largely in the multiple reminders girls and boys receive from adults and from peers as to what are and are not suitable activities for them. A popular alternative explanation may be found. Erik Erikson, in a well-known experimental study of children's toys constructions (1955), also found a difference between the buildings of boys and girls. Typically characteristic of boys' creations were "elaborate buildings," "complicated structures," "channelization of traffic through tunnels and street crossings," and the "erection of high structures." In comparison, girls' constructions typically included "simple walls which merely enclosed interiors, with an emphasis by ornamentation on the vestibular access to the interior," "interiors without walls," and "intrusion into such an interior of a dangerous or mischievous animal or male creature." Erikson explained these differences in the psychodynamics associated with the different sex organs and sex impulses of boys and girls: "In the male the emphasis on the external, the erectable, the instrusive, and the mobile—in the female, on the internal, on the vestibular, on the static, on what is contained and endangered in the interior."

I have no basis to entirely dispute Erikson's symbolic exploration. However, I believe there is a more obvious explanation of why girls' and boys' buildings would differ. Girls are socialized to work with interior spaces and in their play reflect this role, while boys are socialized for adult roles as creators and builders. Erikson should have noticed that girls are encouraged from early on to decorate and to play out social events in interiors, notably in doll houses, while boys are encouraged to build them. While this explanatory discussion cannot be supported by hard evidence, for many persons, reflection on their own early childhood should offer support for these comments.

Effects of Different Environment Experiences on the Development of Girls and Boys

The different amounts of self-directed spatial exploration and opportunities for free manipulation of the environment that seem to characterize girls and boys, especially as they become older, quite probably has serious consequences for the development of certain cognitive abilities (Saegert and Hart, 1976). Very strong evidence exists, through numerous standardized tests of intelligence and ability, that boys, by adolescence, demonstrate greater ability to visualize spatial configurations and to solve problems requiring visual-spatial skills. Interestingly, sex differences are rarely found until about the age of eight. Prior to this time girls are just as likely to excel as are boys; males do not establish a clear superiority in spatial abilities until adolescence (Maccoby and Jacklin, 1974).

Though most of these spatial tests are not considered measures of analytic ability, these differences in spatial ability also seem to be related to differences in mathematical ability, thus giving them increased significance for a child's cognitive growth. Furthermore, male superiority on the visual tests of "field independence" have led others to generalize male superiority even further. A central concept of field independence researchers is articulation or the ability to differentiate figures from ground (Witkin et al 1962). This process is like that involved in any kind of problem solving; a person must project an organization to perform well. Witkin and his colleagues advanced the hypothesis that encouragement of autonomy and support for independent endeavor, together with a secure environment, provide the developmental background for a field independent person. Clearly, from what has been described about boys' greater spatial freedom, and hence freedom to explore and make decisions for themselves, some superior problem solving abilities would be expected.

There is some evidence that spatial abilities are, in part, inherited. Correlational studies revealing stronger relationships between the test scores of mothers and fathers and their male and female offspring support the notion that spatial ability has two components, one genetically sex-linked and the other not. Such studies, however, still conclude that women, though proportionately fewer than men, would display a high level of spatial ability. (One such study estimates that approximately 50 percent of all men and 25 percent of all women show this trait.) As Maccoby and Jacklin (1974) note in their review, this 25 percent of women still far exceeds the proportion of women working in engineering or architecture, for example. It seems that there is a genetic base for the development of spatial abilities but that this base is rarely developed into adult skills, even in the girls and women who possess it. Some evidence already exists that specific training in spatial tasks and visual-spatial skills can do much to improve these abilities in all children, tending to eradicate any initially existing sex differences (see Saegert and Hart review). In addition to specific training, the beneficial effects of support for environmental manipulation and exploration were also indicated by the cross-cultural studies in Kenya mentioned above. [2]

Summary

This paper has argued that the levels of children's use of the outdoors is significantly affected by the different attitudes, rules, and expectations governing the environmental opportunities and experiences of the two sexes. Girls, in particular, are constrained both in their movements and in the nature of their manipulation of the environment. It seems that they are practicing and being prepared for roles in the home and boys for roles outside. It has been noted that environmental competence is not considered appropriate to girls.

It has also been strongly suggested that the very different opportunities given to girls versus boys to freely manipulate the environment affects their spatial abilities and other types of problem solving. Clearly the ability to visualize and analyze spatial relationships is of value generally and is perhaps critical for certain occupations such as engineering and architecture. Its relationship to other skills such as mathematical reasoning and general problem solving makes it even more desirable as an attribute. How this ability develops seems to be a complex process, but it is crucial that we begin to try to understand some of the powerful effects of socialization. It is important that *all* children have the freedom, ability, and confidence to define and carry out their goals and to expand and enrich their lives.

---

[1] To illustrate dramatically how pervasive is the attitude of boys as builders and girls as observers or assistants, naturalistic sequences of film portray dam building on a very large sandbank behind the town's elementary school.

[2] If we wish to truly evaluate the constructive and problem solving abilities of girls as well as boys, we would either have to establish equivalent skills in the girls' world and evaluate boys' and girls' ability with these, or preferably offer a training program in which girls have constructing experiences as much as boys, before being evaluated. This latter approach is shortly to be undertaken in a longitudinal experiment by Saegert and Wolfe of the Environmental Psychology Program and the Center for the Study of Women and Sex Roles of the City University of New York Graduate School.

REFERENCES

Erikson, E. "Sex Differences in Play Construction of Twelve-Year-Old Children," in J.M. Tanner and B. Inhelder, eds., *Discussions on Child Development*, vol. III. London: Tavistock Publications, 1958, pp. 91-132. (Proceedings of the Third Meeting of the World Health Organization Study Group on the Psychobiological Development of the Child, Geneva, 1955.)

Hart, R.A. *Children's Place Experience: A Developmental Study*. New York: Irvington Publishers, 1977.

Landy, David. *Tropical Childhood*. New York: Harper & Row, 1965.

Lewis, M. "State As In Infant-Environment Interaction: An Analysis of Mother-Infant Behavior as a Function of Sex." *Merrill-Palmer Quarterly*, vol. 18, 1972, pp. 95-121.

Maccoby, E.E. and Jacklin, C.N. *The Psychology of Sex Differences.* Stanford, CA: Stanford University Press, 1975.

Munroe, R.L., and Munroe, R.H. "Effect of Environmental Experience on Spatial Ability in an East African Society," *Journal of Social Psychology*, vol. 83, 1971, pp. 15-22.

Nerlove, S.B., Munroe, R.H., and Munroe, R.L. "Effects of Environmental Experience on Spatial Ability: A Replication," *Journal of Social Psychology*, vol. 83, 1971, pp. 3-10.

Saegert, S., and Hart, R.A. "The Development of Environmental Competence in Girls and Boys," in *Women and Society*, P. Burnett, ed. Chicago Maaroufa Press, in press. (Also available from the authors at the Center for Human Environments, CUNY-Graduate School University Center, 33 West 42nd St., New York, NY 10036).

Tindal, M. *The Home Range of Black Elementary School Children: An Exploratory Study in the Measurement and Comparison of Home Range.* Worcester, Mass.: Graduate School of Geography, Clark University, Place Perception Research Report No. 8, 1971.

Witkin, H.A., et al. *Psychological Differentiation.* New York: John Wiley, 1962.

Sex Differences in Use of Outdoor Space • **109**

Parenting

9

Non-Sexist
Parenting at Home
and at School

LETTY COTTIN POGREBIN

Editor, *Ms* Magazine

THE child who enters a preschool day care or nursery school has already been exposed to three or more years of socialization from parents, community, and the culture at large. Research has shown that by the age of three, a child clearly perceives that the male is the source of rewarding power in both the family unit and the larger world. Sexism has already taken root.

But concerned parents and conscientious early childhood educators can undo the limiting and sometimes damaging effects of sexism. In partnership, we can help children expand their views of male and female contributions to society and enlarge their sense of their own potential, whatever their sex, race, or economic class. But first we must understand just how entrenched sex-role stereotypes are in the overall dynamic of child rearing.

The conditioning process begins long before a child is born; it begins with ourselves. Who we are and what we feel about ourselves exist as facts *before* we become parents. And the women who become mothers don't feel especially positive about the basic fact of their femaleness. A Gallup Poll has shown that twelve times more adult women than men wish they were the opposite sex. The male is perceived to be the more valued sex socially, economically, politically, and in every other sphere. If women depreciate themselves, it is no surprise that they depreciate female replicas of themselves.

In one study, Edward Pohlman (1969) determined that pregnant women dream twice as often about having male children and that mothers of female children have postpartum depression almost twice as often as mothers of male children.

The desire for first-born sons is a clear indication of parental sexism. It finds expression in myths and superstitions found in virtually every ethnic subculture. Jewish folk wisdom decrees that a woman eats the heel ends of bread to guarantee a male child. I ate thousands of bread ends in 1965. (I had twin girls.) Friends of mine have reported such practices as making love under a full moon or putting the husband's trousers on the right bed post to insure conception of a boy child.

Once a woman has conceived, it's common to monitor the activity in the uterus. If there's a lot of kicking, a boy is predicted; if the fetus is quiet, of course it will be a girl.

When talking about an unborn child most prospective parents refer to it as "he"—rarely "she" or even "it." The overwhelming majority of parents expecting their first child decide on the male names before debating the female names. And often, during the nine-month-waiting period, parents imagine happy scenarios—a day in the park with their child or a scrubbed little kid going off to school. Ask them the sex of the child in those mind-pictures and more often than not it's a boy. At the moment of birth, according to researcher Michael Lewis (1972), gender is the first thing the mother wants to know. She asks "What is it?" not "Is it healthy? Does it have all its fingers?"

Moments after delivery, the color coding begins. One look in the window of a hospital nursery tells a visitor if the bassinette contains a girl or boy infant. The swaddling clothes are pink or blue. The little identity cards or bracelets are pink or blue. The bands on the cigars father passes out proclaim "It's a boy" or "It's a girl" in pink or blue.

Even language accommodates to gender. Descriptive adjectives, for example, are a sure giveaway to sex-stereotyping. Robin Morgan, the feminist poet (1974), tried an experiment when her newborn baby was in its pram and friends rushed up to ask "What did you have?" On certain days Robin would answer, "A boy." And the friend would inevitably remark, "What a handsome buster!" or "Isn't he a big, strapping baby!" On other days Robin would say, "It's a girl." And the friend would comment, "Oooh, what a sweet little girl!" or "How pretty! How cute and delicate she is!" Same baby; different responses.

In infancy, parental treatment and handling has been found to differ according to the baby's sex. Michael Lewis discovered that in the first 12 weeks, both parents talk and look at girls more, but they hold, touch, rock, and kiss boys more. In another study, it was found that fathers spent an average of 16 to 32 seconds per day with their infants. But during those seconds, a girl was treated with more remoteness, tenderness, or gingerliness and a boy was handled more playfully.

It should not surprise us that when children enter day care or nursery school, girls and boys *seem* so different. Adults have been treating them differently long before teachers ever laid eyes or hands upon them. Every day of their lives young children pick up subtle or flagrant messages that track them into culturally approved sex-roles and sex-appropriate behavior.

Toys, Play, and Games

In a study of North Carolina households (Rheingold and Cook, 1975), the rooms occupied by six-year-old girls contained mostly dolls, dishes, arts and crafts supplies, and passive, quiet games, while six-year-old boys had trucks, blocks, and active sports equipment in their rooms. For an acid test, non-sexist parents ask, "Can I move a six-year-old boy into my daughter's room without changing a thing?" Or vice versa. Parents who wish to raise a full human child, instead of a "masculine" or "feminine" prototype, would be able to do just that. If a child's room contains a wide variety of quality playthings, sturdy, cheerful furnishings (not feminine frills or macho artifacts), books ranging from poetry to adventure tales, sports items *and* rhythm instruments, then that room would be a welcoming, stimulating environment for either sex.

In our present culture, girls' and boys' play styles differ in ways that cannot be considered "separate but equal." Janet Lever (1977) at Northwestern University studied fifth-grade children at play and observed that when play styles differ, it is boys who gain more useful skills. Boys' games encourage outdoor activity, large 'muscle development, healthy cooperation, and competitive and judicial skills that are transferable to adult contexts. Games traditionally played by girls are far more restrictive in the space required, in collaborative efforts, and in their capacity to develop standards for personal achievement. Girls' games, however, provide a superior foundation for empathic behavior, a quality that boys rarely exhibit in their play situations.

While Piaget has noted that no girls' game embodies the challenges presented by a routine (boys') game of marbles, Dr. Spock now acknowledges that (girls') doll play offers emotional and nurturant experiences that should be equally explored by boys. Given this experience, the non-sexist parent is one who abandons dated, rigid notions of boys' or girls' toys and games and instead encourages a great variety of play experiences. Parents can take toys as seriously as children do. Choose children's gifts with care and consciousness. Boycott toys that exploit negative social values or antiquated personifications of female and male roles. Reassure a girl who is hassled for liking baseball or a boy who is ridiculed for liking to cook.

Find out what playthings the child would like but is afraid to request. Discard toy packages that suggest that the item is meant for one sex or the other; rewrap that Handy Andy tool kit with boys pictured on the cover and put the tools in a plain hardware store tool box. Black parents can similarly repackage toys that come illustrated with only white children at play. Children who do not see themselves reflected in a commercial or toy package illustration may feel that toy is not appropriate for them.

Books, Television, Movies

One needn't go so far as to censor the media, though that is a constant temptation to non-sexist parents who bristle at the plotlines, characters, and dialog in the popular culture. Some parents do ban certain programs on grounds of sexism; others help their children learn to get wise to TV's fantasy renditions of family life, economic conditions, and sex-role absurdity. Children can talk back to the television set when it spews nonsense about "Good coffee is grounds for marriage," or "My wife, I think I'll keep her," or housewife's hysteria resulting from "Ring around the collar."

When my daughter was eight years old, she became thoroughly incensed at a Wheaties commercial headlined, "He's ready for Wheaties —he knows he's a man." She wrote a complaint to the company phrased something like, "If you say that one more time, I will not eat another tasty morsel of your cereal, no matter how much I love it. I'm ready for Wheaties, but I know I'm a woman." The company answered with Form Letter B detailing how market analysts had determined Wheaties is a "masculine" cereal. But, as you may have noticed, eventually the commercials were "desexed,"—and my daughter is convinced her letter helped bring about change.

Sexism in books, TV, or movies can be as insidious as racism or violence because it is a powerful reinforcement of the worst excesses and myths of the patriarchal culture. Discussions between parents and children can raise all the issues and allow children to develop standards of their own that will last long after parental censorship is forgotten.

Family roles and policy

Studies of young children indicate that adult male and female roles are not seen as complementary, no matter how much adults may proclaim an equal division of labor. For example, a person who *fixes* is perceived as more glamorous than a person who *cleans*. The parent who goes out to an oppressive, routinized factory job is seen by a child as more important and productive than the parent who does the oppressive job of dish washing and floor scrubbing. With the aid of the media, children attach differential value to kinds of work and behavior and to the sex of the person most often identified with each.

Where relaxation of domestic sex roles is concerned, parental intervention is crucial. It doesn't cost money, and it doesn't take a lot of time. If laundry needs folding, a child can fold alongside daddy instead of mommy. A little girl who fixes a leaky faucet with her mother will not need a doctrinaire lecture about female self-sufficiency. Children pick up subliminal messages about adult versatility and competence when both parents are involved in school activities, sports events, bath-time, or story-time, when each parent is seen in the driver's seat of the family car, or when both parents take obvious responsibility for the household finances.

In the single parent household, more conscious efforts may be required to present a child with opposite sex-role models, and friends, relatives, and community may have to be relied upon for example and inspiration. A visit to a man tailor or chef persuades a child that men can —and do—sew or cook. A chat with a policewoman or becoming the patient of a female pediatrician can reinforce the assurance that "girls can be anything they want to be."

Awareness of parental policy toward discipline and privileges also may yield surprising differences along sex lines. A double standard in corporal or verbal punishment or expectations of cleanliness, courtesy, bravery, or independence is proof that one sex or the other is being favored or penalized. In household chores, for example, boys are commonly expected to take out garbage and mow lawns, while girls are asked to set the table or do the dishes—thereby creating hard and fast notions about "women's work" and "man-sized jobs." A 16-year-old girl had a valid complaint when she was prohibited from staying out until midnight after her 15-year-old brother was permitted that privilege. Parental values should be sex-blind and supportable by a more convincing rubric than, "Boys don't . . ." or "Girls shouldn't . . ."

By the same token, the nature of the relationship *between* the parents themselves may imprint a child with lifelong perceptions about the way females and males behave together. "Don't disturb your father, he's reading" is a mother's bid for consideration on the father's behalf. "Don't disturb your mother, she's painting (or thinking, or sewing)" would be a similar acknowledgement by the father that he respects his wife's enterprise, whatever it may be.

This kind of "raised consciousness" may create self-consciousness at first, but it's well worth the transitional awkwardness and readjustments, particularly for developing self-esteem of little girls and their images of their own perfectable futures. I'm thinking of a little girl who heard her mother describe her own younger days, when she was a tennis player, went mountain climbing, and worked in a chemistry lab, all before the child was born. The little girl listened to the exciting account, looked wistfully at her mother, and said, "Gee mom, I wish I knew you sooner."

Research shows that regardless of socio-economic class and background, all mothers expected their sons to be independent, responsible, resourceful, and vocationally motivated. But with the exception of a minority of educated, upper-income households, few of these same character traits were encouraged by mothers of daughters. Perhaps most mothers understood too well the folly of raising female expectations in a world designed to frustrate female striving. But now there is a new vista and new hope for change in all the diverse areas of girls' and women's lives—and in the lives of the boys and men with whom they live, learn, and work.

Educators are in the unique position of fostering and nourishing those changes during the formative "magic" years of childhood. But in some cases, for example, in my children's nursery school, the parents happened to be more sensitive to sexism than the teachers. Several feminist parents got together to present a seminar on non-sexist books, toys, attitudes, and so on. We exchanged with the larger parent body lists of recommended books and movies. Several teachers attended the seminar and showed enthusiastic, open-minded responses to our "non-professional" presentation. They added their own suggestions or used the opportunity to confess candidly that, "I never realized how I've stereotyped my four-year-olds," or "I think I'll get rid of the boy-girl labels on the dress-up clothes boxes," or "Gee, we have dozens of those sexist books right on our shelves."

A wonderful dialogue had begun. The teachers were grateful for the parents' initiative—after all, they had been immersed in teaching while some of us had been immersed in feminism, and they were pleased to benefit from our expertise. At the same time, they improved on our basic consciousness-raising methods by translating ideas and enlightenment into classroom-applicable concepts. The teachers were quick to draw upon the occupational resources of the parent group.

One mother who was a doctor brought her medical paraphernalia into a class of fives, and without blatant bulletins, the children picked up on the fact that this was a mommy *and* a doctor! A woman lawyer came into my son's third-grade class and organized a moot court case with eight-year-old lawyers, jury, and judge. A kindergarten group went to a bread bakery where men were wearing aprons and covered in flour. A teacher needn't restrict role models to male and females in non-traditional jobs—but if you have a mother who's a firefighter, don't let her get away.

Non-Sexist Parenting • **119**

In non-academic school affairs, it very often seems to fall to the mother to act as liaison. Non-sexist parent groups will not designate a "class mother" but a "class parent" and will actively seek fathers' involvement with father-daughter as well as father-son and mother-daughter activities. At our school street fair, we had a man storyteller, a woman auctioneer, a man who painted clown faces on the kids, and a woman who gave pony rides with a rented pony. These are some obvious, easy ways to enrich children's perceptions of the human potential, human variety, and human worth of women and men alike.

The more difficult problems remain. A coalition between parents and educators, no matter how energized and committed, cannot by itself solve the big problems. To deliver adequate health care, to offer quality child care alternatives, to guarantee employment and thereby dignity to all who seek work, to provide support systems for burdened parents, to view child care programs as a child's right, not a hand-out to force the poor off welfare, and to integrate the resources of senior citizens and young adults into the texture of small children's lives—all this requires full-scale social reorganization and a revision of national priorities.

While engaged in the larger struggle, we cannot lose sight of the individual—the one or two or ten lives that we can touch with our own. I'm convinced we have to enhance children's *todays* while working on our common *tomorrows*. In the arduous battle against sexism, we can keep in mind the kindergarten class in Pittsburgh whose members were asked what they each want to be when they grow up (Lever, 1977).

There was the predictable round of answers—the boys wanted to be astronauts, truck drivers, or firemen, and the girls dreamed of becoming ballerinas, librarians, or stewardesses. But then there was a twist to the query. The children were asked, "What would you want to be if you were the opposite sex?"

One little boy said, "Well, I guess if I was a girl, then I'd have to grow up and be nothing."

And the first little girl who was asked what she'd be if she were a boy, answered with bright eyes, "Ah, if I were a boy, I would grow wings and fly across the city."

That little girl's answer symbolizes, for me, the goal of non-sexist parenting. And that little boy's response is a reminder of how far we have yet to go before American males cease to pity and patronize American females. While parents cannot rear their children in a cultural vacuum, we can give our daughters and sons that vision of flight and freedom and the conviction that all things are possible. We can help them grow wings!

REFERENCES

Lever, Janet, "Ms. Gazette, (new coverage)" *Ms.* February, 1977.

Lewis, M. "Parents and Children: Sex Role Development," *School Review,* February 1972.

Personal interview, Morgan, Robin, 1974.

Pohlman, E. *The Psychology of Birth Planning.* Cambridge, MA: Schenkman Publishing Co., 1969.

Rheingold, Harriet L., and Cook, Kaye V. "The Contents of Boys' and Girls' Rooms as an Index of Parents Behavior," *Child Development,* Vol. 46 1975, pp. 459-463.

10

Problems and Priorities of Poor, Culturally Different Parents

DR. HELEN RODRIGUEZ-TRÍAS
Department of Pediatrics
Lincoln Hospital

I'VE had a very hard time deciding what I should touch upon, and I think my difficulty flows from two areas. One is the area of personal experience, of having brought up four children under relatively difficult circumstances in the colonial setting of Puerto Rico, which is, in a way, a patriarchy institutionalized for a whole nation rather than for just a family. A colony fosters dependence; it fosters all kinds of traits of the oppressed such as docility and humility, but it does not ever foster self-defense not even any sense of self or self-oriented values. To me, that has been a very painful experience.

In addition, my own daily work reminds me of my own experience since it puts me in contact with men and women who are trying to raise families in a ghetto, which is perhaps like the lowest layer of the colonial setting. It's a very difficult enterprise, really, and I think we can't speak to what we will do in our interventions in terms of the one-to-one relationship or the small programs we have here or there without looking at the structure of the society itself, and without perhaps questioning the brutally hierarchical nature of this society.

A Child-Hating Society

We must begin to look at parenting, not just in terms of sex roles but in terms of parenting—period. By parenting, I mean the effective intervention of parents that protects children so that they may survive. This protection is essential for I'm convinced we're living in a child-hating society. I must say that. I am convinced ours is a human beings-hating society, but, of course, some groups of human beings are more vulnerable than others. Children happen to be very vulnerable. Old people happen to be very vulnerable. Certain minority groups happen to be very vulnerable. This is where we see the effects of hatred at its worst. We need only look at the allocation of resources for child care, child health, child education, or any other services for children to know that there is more than just "benign neglect." In a place where perhaps only five percent of the children who should be in day care are in day care, day care funds are cut! In a place where only 15 percent of the children who were qualified by law to be in Head Start programs were actually in Head Start programs, Head Start is being cut back. In some communities where only 50 percent of the children have had even their primary immunizations, child health stations are being cut. Therefore, I find it hard not to think that this is a child-hating society.

We need to look no further than the statistics on infant mortality and those we know on child abuse, including the pervasive and highly destructive sexual abuse, mainly of girls but also of boys, to know that the societal abuse and neglect of children takes its toll daily. It's not that we're going to say, "Okay, we're going to change the world," but in the development of our programs in education, or health, or whatever system we are involved in as workers, we have to keep the social framework in mind. We have to address ourselves to it. I don't think we can just push it away and say, "Well, I'm teaching my little class here very comfortably," or, "I'm running my little clinic, and it's really a humane little clinic."

We know that hatred for children and other people is inversely proportional to social class. I'm sure the Rockefeller children and other upper class children are not quite as hated as the Perez children who happen to be living in the South Bronx. But, like sexism, it affects all classes. The child abuse phenomenon is, by no means, a phenomenon only of the poor. This has been well documented. There is a tremendous incidence of underreporting in the most affluent groups, but, nevertheless, abuse exists. Of course, the poor have less recourse to counseling services, nursery schools or the housekeepers than the more affluent. Poor parents may be hauled into court, their children placed in a foster home nearly as brutal as the one they came from, and the whole case written off as one more incidence of the inability of people of certain class origins to parent—a comment made over and over again.

To overcome the attitudes that make for a punitive approach to child care, we developed a program to sensitize staff to problem situations that occur in homes that may lead to child abuse. The objective was to sensitize people to the fact that parenting is *at best* a difficult task and that within certain settings, where people have to stand from five o'clock in the morning on the welfare line to get a check, or where people have to run out to buy the 50 cents worth of something for dinner and have no place to leave the children, or where people who wait three hours in an emergency room have had to leave the kids alone at home, parenting is seen in its most hazardous form. Part of what we tried to develop with pre-med and medical students was an awareness of the many problems faced by people who are bringing up their children under difficult circumstances. Parenting *is* difficult, and members of a health care team or workers within a health care system have to be sensitive to that—so, please, do not become bad parents who are constantly scolding other people and telling them how terribly they do their job. Rather, see yourselves in their place and become sensitive enough to be supportive.

People have resources. In this child-hating society, there have been enough child lovers to save us and to save others, so that I think there *are* resources. There are human resources of love and caring and knowledge and strength. They're there in the South Bronx as well as they are everywhere else. This is what we have to begin to build on. But we can't build on it unless we have raised our own consciousness to understand our role as a supportive one and to recognize those positive elements of strength that are already there.

Incorporating Parenting into the Curriculum

I see parenting as an occupation that is very much in crisis and that certainly needs an all-out rescue effort. I see one of the possibilities of rescue lying within the educational system. In the educational system, it is possible to build-in parenting as part of the curriculum. This is possible in the same way that people have fought for and have won the inclusion of sex education.

An idea that has been carried out in some places is to attach day care centers to junior high schools as part of their own curriculum or work-study program. Junior high school students come in and care for children in a well supervised environment. They learn about child development within the day care setting. I think this is a marvelous way to teach child care because it not only provides the kind of experience that may be missing, particularly from those who have lost the extended family, but it also allows child care to be taught in a different way. The day care setting may allow a breakthrough from some of the family molds that may be fossilized and stultifying.

This breakthrough is very much needed to eliminate some of the sex-role imprinting that is stereotyped. The experiences may very well serve to deter young people from jumping into parenthood out of other frustrations, or the need to prove their maleness, or their femaleness, or their ability to be independent, or whatever other reasons teenagers have for having children. The contacts may be a deterrent simply because the young people have been responsible for children and have learned the difficulties that a parental relationship entails, something that, again, was perhaps previously learned in the extended family but is now all too often missing from the social setting. Such a program is one way of breaking through within the educational system that might be very important for the parents of the future.

Input from Different Cultural Groups

Frequently raised questions I heard in response to Barbara Bowman's remarks (see chapter one) is, "How about other cultures? How about Puerto Ricans, or how about the many different cultural groups among black people, because certainly theirs is not a homogeneous group, or the many cultural groups there may be among the Spanish-speaking populations in the United States? How about the Asian groups?" All these contribute to the *very rich*, varied, cultural heritage that is the United States. How does one work through on that?

To me, the way to approach these concerns is the way one would approach any challenges raised by a multicultural society, which is to obtain the viewpoints and contributions of the different cultural groups. I don't think that sex-role differentiation is any different from any other problem. The question would not even arise if there were multicultural representation in all our service institutions. If, in the educational system, we had incorporated as teachers and as educators representative numbers of all the varied cultures, cultural diversity problems wouldn't arise. Each culture would know how to begin to solve problems with the sensitivity of its own group. We wouldn't even have to talk about cross-cultural experiences, or cultural awareness, or all the labels that have recently been trotted out because the health services agency legislation would require that this be built in or legislation for school funding would require that cultural awareness be built in. All of which is essentially an artificial way of developing awareness.

Once more, I say this has to be an arena of struggle. We can't just be content to obtain a few more skills in dealing with people who are different from ourselves. I think we have to struggle for the *inclusion* of people who are different from ourselves within the seats of power, within the seats of decision-making in the educational system, in the Head Start programs, in day care, in the health care systems, and in all other institutions. The development of sensitivity has to accompany the struggle for total participation.

But meanwhile, what do we do? We don't have proportionate numbers of Puerto Rican teachers in New York to teach the increased number of children under 18 years of age who, in the inner-city, happen to be Puerto Rican. What about the teachers who *are* teaching? How about the human potential that is present there? I think they have to work hand in hand with people from the community. I believe there has to be a complete involvement of parents, and I think that the question of whether sexism, racism, or whatever comes first, becomes a moot question, because people set up their priorities as they see the needs at a given moment.

I believe that black parents' concern or Puerto Rican parents' concern about the destruction of their children, both boys and girls, is a very legitimate one. We can talk about the role that sexism and sex stereotyping plays within that destruction, but we can't forget about the role that the hierarchical structuring of power plays vis-a-vis both boys and girls. Therefore, we must be very attentive to parents' concerns. If a boy is being weeded out because he's raucous, or a girl is being weeded out later on because she doesn't show any initiative, I think the concern must be for both boys and girls.

We must attend to the power relationships, because I don't think that it much matters whether I'm stereotyped as a good cook, as long as being a good cook doesn't mean that I'm going to be scorned, looked down upon, made to cook three meals a day every day of my life, and left at home without a penny—in other words, oppressed, in the myriad of ways there are of oppressing.

Occupational differences are not the problem; they are only part of it. The root of the problem is the kind of prestige and the amount of power that goes with an occupation. Our self-images do have a great deal to do with our ability to use power and with our ability to develop to our full potential—there is already an existing power structure that is independent of our self-images. We may demand equal pay for equal work but that will not of itself adequately reward those who do different kinds of work according to their abilities or inclinations. Their rewards must improve too. Equal pay for equal work, yes, but also more equal pay for different kinds of work.

11

Fathers
Are Parents
Too

JAMES LEVINE

Author of *Who Will Raise the Children?
New Options for Fathers (and Mothers)*

I'D like to share with you a different perspective on the issue of parenting. What'd I'd like to do is pick up on Ms. Bowman's points. I think she very rightly suggested that we're dealing with complex issues. When dealing with non-sexist education in the classroom or in the home, we're always dealing with issues that involve every aspect of our society. What I'd like to suggest, however, is that it's precisely because of that complexity that we can't afford to be simplistic or reductive in talking about those issues. We have to think in broader terms. We have to be able to think about social change beyond non-sexist curricula in the classroom.

I'd like to broaden our discussion, hopefully broaden our vision, by including a group that's very often left out of discussions about parenthood or non-sexist education. I'd like to talk a little bit about the context in which parents are told what roles are appropriate for men and women, in which parent educators are told what we should teach parents to do. I'd like to suggest briefly just how pervasive the exclusion of fatherhood—the exclusion of any idea that men could or should be involved with young children—is in our society, what its consequences are, and how we might change the context, to some extent, for parenthood. Let me start by giving a couple of incidences of the pervasiveness of that exclusion of fathers.

One of the books I know that high school educators have very often on their shelves is by Haim Ginott, *Between Parent and Child* (1975), a best-selling book in this country. The advice that Dr. Ginott has for parents is this:

> In the modern family, many men find themselves involved in mothering activities, such as feeding, diapering, and bathing a baby. Although some men welcome these new opportunities for closeness, there is the danger that the baby may end up with two mothers, rather than with a mother and a father.

I could go on and give you three hundred, maybe four hundred, similar examples. I could pick up practically any child-rearing manual, except the revised Spock, and find similar quotes, so this isn't just one small incident. Those notions are institutionalized throughout society.

Let me give you another example from the courts. In 1971 a standard handbook on family law (Rorris, 1971) written for practicing attorneys in Minnesota gave the following advice:

> Except in very rare cases, the father should not have the custody of the minor children of the parties. He is usually unqualified psychologically and emotionally, nor does he have the time and care to supervise the children. A lawyer not only does an injustice to himself, but he is unfair to his client, to the state, and to society if he gives any encouragement to the father that he should have custody of the children. A lawyer who encourages his client to file for custody, unless it is one of the classic exceptions, has difficulty collecting his fees, has a most unreasonable client, has taken the time of the court and the welfare agencies involved, and has put a burden on his legal brethren.

Where do these ideas come from? That's very difficult to trace. I would like to suggest, however, that, in part, some of these ideas come from an old research tradition in this country, which looks only at mothers and not fathers. The dominant notion in our society is that kids need mothers in some special way, that mothers are the only people capable of taking care of their young. It goes back to Freud and beyond, to folklore before modern science. Modern science has institutionalized that idea in the work of Bowlby and the research tradition that followed him. Consider, for example, that there haven't been studies until very, very recently of fathers. It's as if they don't exist at all. There was a study done in 1958 called *The Changing American Parent* (Miller and Swanson). Five hundred and eighty-two parents were surveyed; all were mothers. There is a classic book called *Patterns of Child Rearing* (Sears et al, 1957). Three hundred and seventy-nine parents were interviewed; all were mothers. When Blood and Wolfe wrote *Husband and Wives: The Dynamics of Married Living* (1960), they interviewed 909 *mothers.*

My favorite study is one that really was a pathbreaker; in 1969 Pedersen and Robson did a study called "Father Participation in Infancy." It was the first study to acknowledge that men might have something to do with infants. There's a footnote in this study in which the authors apologize for the fact that maybe they didn't have the courage of their convictions, that in doing their study they didn't speak to any fathers; they spoke only to mothers about father participation in infancy. They say, in part, that may have been because they were unable or unwilling to rearrange their own research working schedules so that they could spend time talking to or observing fathers.

Now this almost unbelievable research tradition is starting to change to some extent. All these studies about infants' attachments to their mothers had been based on looking at infants and their mothers. The mother walks out of the room, the child cries—separation protest. Everybody says it's important for kids to have their mothers, and only their mothers. Well, nobody ever put a father in the room.

In 1972 a researcher at Harvard named Milton Kotelchuck said, "That doesn't make any sense." He did a study (1972) that included fathers, and he discovered a very curious thing—when fathers walked out of the room, children cried! In a sense what Kotelchuck did, and what some other scientists are doing, is discovering a new creature. It doesn't lactate; it doesn't have a uterus, but it shows a surprisingly warm relationship with its young. And its young seem to respond to it as well!

I'm trying to suggest that we really need a whole new consciousness, a new discovery—not just in research, but in the courts and in the child-rearing manuals. In talking about parenting and non-sexist parenting, we have to persuade our institutions to recognize the existence of "the other parent."

I would like to point quickly, hopefully suggestively, to the future. What would we have to do to change things? It's very disheartening often to feel how thoroughly ingrained our patterns of child rearing are, how sexist the patterns of parenting really are. I don't think things can be changed quickly. I think they're very related to economic conditions. But I think there are some ways to look at these issues and some areas to consider, not only in the classroom, not only in terms of exposing young children to images of men taking care of kids, and not only to including men as teachers when they're competent and capable in the classroom.

Let's look at the life cycle of a father. Most of you probably are familiar with Lamaze and husband-coached child birth. In fact, however, that is still a relatively rare phenomenon. In many hospitals throughout the country, men are still not allowed to participate at the birth of their children. I discovered, in a rural town in Minnesota, a retired postal clerk who was sending money to support a law case in Louisiana that was trying to allow men into the delivery room of a hospital receiving federal funds. This man's son had participated at the birth of his child, and the grandfather was so moved by this and felt that he had been deprived of something that was so vital, that he was trying to support others. I'd like to suggest that there are many hospitals out there that deny men the experience of participating at the birth of their children. In my own case, before our second child was born, (We were very progressive; we were going to do Lamaze) when checking out the hospital, we found that I would be allowed to attend at the birth, that I was allowed to visit maybe for an hour or two hours a day, and then I could come and pick up Joan and the baby about three days later. I was pushed right out of the parenting situation. So I'd like to suggest that hospital practices are an area where change is needed.

After fathers and mothers come home from the hospital, I'd like to suggest that we need social policies in this country that would really be supportive of families, supportive of the opportunities of men and women to share in caring for their young children. Sweden has a marvelous approach to this. It has something called parental insurance. It's drawn from social security, and it allows either or both parents to stay home for up to eight months at 90 percent of pre-birth salary. What that means is that the mother can stay home for eight months or the father can stay home for eight months, or they can split it five and three, or they could both work part-time, and both be involved at home more fully. Sweden not only has this policy, but it is trying to create an incentive for men to become involved. An extra month will be added to this leave if men participate.

Let me look at another broader area. The structure of work in our society makes it difficult for men to be involved. For instance, usually only fathers who are unemployed, voluntarily or not, are able to be involved as class parents. I'd like to suggest changes that would allow men to be involved and women to be involved with their kids, and both still be employed. I think what we need is more flexible-time opportunities, more permanent part-time work, both for men and for women.

Again, let me give you an example of what I mean. In an experiment a couple of years ago, Norway tried to figure out a policy for family life in the future, recognizing the fact that families were undergoing changes and that this applied not only to women's roles but to men's roles as well. It implemented something called the work-sharing experiment. It permitted parents of young children to work no less than 16 and no more than 28 hours per week. That meant they could have active working lives and still be involved more fully with their young children. This is done also in conjunction with the development of day care, nurseries, and programs outside the home. One of the big questions was, "What is this going to do to the employer? Is productivity going to flag?" It didn't. All the studies with which I'm familiar have shown that there aren't reductions in productivity when employees shift to a part-time or flex-time type of structure.

I've been traveling around the country and telling people about this notion. When I make this point about restructuring working time, one of the questions is, "Well, you couldn't do that. If you tried to do that tomorrow, the whole structure would cave in. It's impossible. We're never going to be able to achieve that." I'd like to suggest that these changes will come about slowly, but it's important for us to have the consciousness to start thinking about radical changes in many of our structures, so that many of our institutions will be able to fully include men and women in parenting and in fuller lives outside the home.

One of the people said, "What would happen if—take the president of the bank—what if he (and it was "he" that was used) had to run out of a meeting at 2 o'clock to go home and take care of the kids?" I'd like to suggest that if the Secretary of Defense in our country were in that position, it wouldn't be such a bad thing.

REFERENCES

Blood, Robert O., and Wolfe, Donald M. *Husbands and Wives: The Dynamics of Married Living.* New York: Free Press, 1960.

Ginott, Haim, Dr. *Between Parent and Child.* New York: Macmillan, 1975, pp. 168-169.

Kotelchuck, Milton. "The Nature of the Child's Tie to His Father," PhD. dissertation, Harvard University, April 1972, p. 141.

Miller, Daniel R. and Swanson, Guy E. *The Changing American Parent.* New York: Wiley, 1958.

Pedersen, Frank A., and Robson, Kenneth S. "Father Participation in Infancy," *American Journal of Orthopsychiatry,* vol. 39, No. 3, April 1969, pp. 467-468.

Rorris, James F. "Separation Agreements-Support for the Spouse and Minor Children," *Minnesota-Family Law, Minnesota Practice Manual 50.* Minneapolis: University of Minnesota, 1971, p. 75.

Sears, Robert R., Maccoby, Eleanor E., and Levin, Harry, *Patterns of Child Rearing.* Evanston, ILL: Row, Peterson, 1957.

Roundup
of Perspectives

12

Sex Role and Human Culture

DR. PATRICK C. LEE

Associate Professor of Education
Teachers College, Columbia University

THE Conference on Non-Sexist Early Childhood Education generated so many diverse threads of ideology, feelings, and practical concerns over how we can work more effectively with children that I am unequal to my assigned task of pulling them all together. Thus, I would like to focus on one thematic thread, which was introduced by Barbara Bowman and importantly influenced the direction of much of the ensuing dialogue. The theme is the relationship of sex role to the total fabric of human culture.

Frederick Douglass once said that to understand one must, "stand under." As a white, middle class male, no longer young, but not yet old —in socio-political terms, in the prime of my life—perhaps I have stood too much over and too little under. But let me now "stand under" . . . and try to understand.

Without question, sex role is an important dimension of human culture. To meddle with sex role is to meddle with human culture—and when one meddles with human culture, one meddles with human survival—these are undeniable truisms.

Two Interaction Models

As I see it, there are two models of interaction between culture and the rate of sex-role change that are of interest here. In the first model, sex-role change moves ahead too quickly, thus threatening to throw the carefully wrought interconnections of culture into disorder and chaos. The second model is the converse of the first. In this model, sex role threatens cultural integrity by changing too slowly.

I think that the second model applies to North American middle class society. I will argue strongly for this proposition—that is, that change in the sex roles is proceeding too slowly, that the traditional sex roles have become nostalgic anchoring points in an era that closed down at the end of the Second World War, that they linger on like ghosts from the past while American society careens into the future.

But before I pursue that point, let me speculate for a moment about the first model. Several minority group representatives have argued that they are being asked to move too fast and that this conflicts with their own sense of cultural priorities. I think that what they are saying is that the effects of racism and poverty have been more damaging to minority group women than the effects of sexism. Thus, they feel they must close ranks with their men and children and pull together. Only as the legacy of racism and poverty wanes, can the problem of sexism be confronted. Obviously this does not mean that minority group women are insensitive to sexism as a form of human oppression. Their presence at the Conference indicated their very real sensitivity to sexism. It only means that they trust and need their men more than they trust and need white, middle class women. This does not automatically exclude them from the ranks of feminism. It only means that they are charting an independent course, which touches base with middle class feminism where it can, but goes its own way where it must.

However oppressed minority women are today and have been in history, they have never been *trivialized* to the same degree and in the same manner as middle class women. They have been asked to do too much, and they have been given too little in return. But they have at least been *necessary*—they have seldom been playthings in the context of their home cultures. As such, they have held relatively higher status in their subcultures than white middle class women have for the last one hundred years held in their subculture. Let me further speculate that minority group women have held their relatively valued status specifically because of larger American society's systematic degradation and humiliation of their men. This is quite different from the middle class situation in which women are, among other things, trying to protect themselves *from* their men.

Now I fully recognize the danger in speculations such as these. First, there is great diversity among minority subcultures and to seek one formula that pretends to apply to several subcultures defies logic as well as prudence. Second, there is almost inherent rashness to one such as myself claiming to understand simply because I have volunteered to "stand under." But I wanted to speculate on a matter that puzzled this Conference greatly. Even if the substance of my speculation is incorrect, minority group people may still find the first model of cultural interaction with sex role a useful one. And it is in this spirit that I offer both the speculations and the model.

Let me move now to terrain where I have a surer footing. The second interaction model, which holds that sex role is changing too slowly, is the one that applies to middle class American culture. There are four cultural vehicles that allow for interaction between the sexes: courtship practices, marriage, family, and division of labor. These vehicles are present in all cultures, but their form varies from culture to culture. Since they determine how the sexes interact, they determine the nature of sex role. My contention is that through massive changes in technology, economics, means of social organization, and socio-political awareness, these four vehicles are themselves changing rapidly and radically. Since they determine the form and substance of sex role, when they change, sex roles must also change. If the sex roles fail to change—and isn't this the basic question being considered here?—then the threat they pose to cultural integrity and human survival is not one of dashing ahead too quickly, but of lagging behind too stubbornly.

Technological Changes

A few words about technological change. . . . Developments in the technologies of work, the household, contraception, and longevity have had far reaching effects on the functional differences between the sexes. Labor-saving machinery and automated systems in the world of work have eliminated the advantage of male strength and size in many industries and occupations, thus tending to create jobs that are not typed for one sex or the other. Labor-saving devices in the household have reduced the amount of time and energy middle and working class women need for their traditional domestic responsibilities. Many women use the resulting surplus time for employment outside the home or for self-improvement and education, often combining these functions with raising families. Since 1940, for example, the number of working mothers in the United States has increased eightfold and they now constitute almost 40 percent of all working women.° The technology of birth control, particularly the contraceptive pill, has freed many women from the burden of repeated pregnancies and parents from the inevitability of large families. Moreover, it has given the average women a degree of control over the consequences of her own sexuality, which was unknown in the past, thereby contributing immeasurably to the revolution in sexual mores and to the gradual breakdown of double standards of sexual behavior. Advances in the technology of medical care and nutrition have increased longevity dramatically during the twentieth century. Both men and women are living longer and have more leisure years after retiring from their work and homemaking responsibilities. Since old age is a life stage in which sex differentiation tends to wane, enhanced longevity means that our society now has relatively more people who place relatively less emphasis on differences between the sexes.

Regarding economic change, since 1950 the number of women in the world of work has almost doubled, until they now make up about 40 percent of the total labor force in the United States. While the domestic technology referred to above might tend to create a "boredom push" of women out of the home into work, it appears that the more important factor has been "income pull." Nearly two-thirds of American working women are single, divorced, widowed, separated, or have husbands

---

°Facts and figures cited here and in the following paragraphs are taken from recent official reports of the Women's Bureau of the U.S. Department of Labor and the Census Bureau of the U.S. Department of Commerce.

who earn less than $7,000 a year. It is safe to conjecture that a large percentage of the remaining third are also working because the standard of living of their families, while not marginal, requires two incomes. Men continue to be the main source of income for American families and continue to work more on the average than women do. But, due to the increasingly technical nature of many contemporary jobs, men require more pre-employment training and/or educational preparation. Consequently, males are entering the job market later than in the past.

Moreover, changes in technology and in labor practice have made work weeks shorter and retirement ages earlier than they were in the past. This has had the net effect of reducing the amount of time men work relative to their life span and, coupled with the increase of working women, has reduced the discrepancy between men and women in sheer amount of time spent at gainful employment. In other words, the experience of formal employment outside the home, once almost the exclusive preserve of men, has become something men and women increasingly share. None of this is to say that there has not been discrimination against women in the world of work; it's only to say that, whatever inequities continue to exist, men are working less, women are working more, and the experience of work no longer existentially separates men and women to the degree that it once did. In fact, to the degree that capitalism reduces labor to an object commodity, it tends ultimately to homogenize the sexes.

Changes in the Family and Marriage

The last two decades have also seen great changes in the family, the basic unit of social organization in Western society. The typical American family is increasingly nuclear and neo-local, in sharp contrast to the traditional extended family, which tended to cluster in one community or region. In the absence of the extended familial support system, there has been a convergence of function between husbands and wives, which commonly results in role overlap and, occasionally, role reversal. The movement of women into the labor force suggests that Talcott Parsons' (1955) classic designation of women as "expressive" and men as "instrumental" no longer holds. Women are increasingly assuming instrumental functions as they pursue the family's interests in the outside world. Conversely, as James Levine commented earlier (see chapter 11), recently emerged concern about "fathering" among men indicates that they are taking on more of the expressive function of maintaining affective ties within the family.

Another phenomenon having a major effect on the integrity of the nuclear family is the increased incidence of divorce. In the United States in 1975 there was one divorce for every 2.1 marriages, a dramatic gain of 85 percent over 1960, when the ratio of divorce to marriage was 1 to 3.9. There are now approximately one million divorces and over half a million legal separations annually in the United States, which involve well over one million dependent children each year.

The accelerated divorce rate is creating two alternative kinds of families. Divorced people who remarry, and most do, are forming a type of nuclear family that has a shifting membership and one in which children often have strong ties to a parent, usually their biological father, who belongs to another family. Those who do not remarry are joining the burgeoning ranks of single-parent families. There are now over six and a half million single-parent families in the United States, which include 14 percent of all American youngsters below 18 years of age. Moreover, during the period 1955 to 1975, single-parent families were increasing at almost twice the rate of two-parent families.

It is evident, then, that novel family forms are increasingly prevalent and that the traditional complementarity of sex-divided labor no longer holds in two-parent nuclear families and is simply dysfunctional in single-parent families, where the remaining parent, usually the mother, must assume both parental roles. As mentioned earlier, the family is one of the major societal vehicles for interface between the sexes; thus changes in its basic structure must inevitably lead to changes in the ways the sexes interact. These, in turn, can be expected to yield new profiles of functional sex differences and similarities, that is, new sex roles.

Marriage customs are also undergoing marked change. They are changing as a result of the interaction between the technology of contraception and the economics of female employment. As Selma Greenberg remarked (see chapter 2), widespread earning power among women has provided them a degree of financial independence enjoyed by only a select few in the past. Contraceptive methods designed for female use (as opposed to those designed for males) have given women the prerogative of disassociating their sexual behavior from pregnancy and childbirth, thus freeing them from traditional social and biological constraints on their sexuality. The relative availability of pre-marital and extra-marital sexual partners for both men and women, in turn, has tended to reduce the importance of sex as an incentive to marriage, contributing to the present American trend, evolving over the last 15 years, toward marrying at a later age.

Economic self-reliance has also reduced the need for women to marry in order to be supported by a man. In fact, a women's real or potential earning power has become a new criterion for female desirability since the availability of two incomes is often a prerequisite to the maintenance of an acceptable standard of living. For example, a working wife is an indispensable asset to many men who require long preparation for professional careers; the wives in such arrangements provide support for their husbands as an investment in the economic stability of their own futures. Interestingly enough, these marriages upset the traditional formula in which the man offered material support in return for exclusive sexual rights to the woman. In many contemporary marriages, the reverse almost seems to be the case, at least during the early years of the marriage, and it is for this reason that I have used this example.

Among highly educated and/or talented people there is an increasing incidence of dual profession and childless "companionate" marriages, in which the functional distinctions between the two sexes are practically non-existent. These marital arrangements are relatively infrequent, even by contemporary standards, but they are often accorded high visibility by the news media, thus tending to pull the broad spectrum of middle and working class arrangements in more "progressive" directions.

Effects of These Cultural Changes

All these cultural changes, contracted into the relatively brief time span of one or, at most, one and a half generations, have had an enormous impact on the respective psychologies of the sexes. One must ask, "How do people *feel* and *think* about these discontinuities in their experience? How do they feel about themselves as men and women?" Doubtlessly, the changes have involved psychological dislocations for both sexes. But such dislocations can be viewed positively, as opening new opportunities for personal growth, and negatively, as closing down familiar routes to personal identity.

For example, one effect of these changes has been to blur the accepted boundaries between conventional male and female functions. Women are surrendering their traditional expressive primacy in the family and men their instrumental primacy in the world of work and community affairs. It is difficult to imagine that these respective primacies are being abandoned with total equanimity, for, whatever constraints they placed on individual development in the past, at least they offered structure and a sense of order to people's lives. The breakdown of familiar structures is usually accompanied by a degree of anxiety, which may account for the resistance among many men and women to change the roles of the two sexes. It may also account for the tentative exhilaration felt by many ordinary people, particularly by women, who sense that new options, once closed to them, are now open.

Contrary to what Selma Greenberg has said, I may add that another effect of these changes has been the reduction of segregation between the sexes. In the past there has been amazingly little opportunity for the formation of socially accepted relationships between the sexes outside the culturally sanctioned vehicles of courtship, marriage, and family. But today relationships based on friendship, convenience, and occupational interdependence are increasing in the working world, educational institutions, social clubs, the political arena, and a variety of other cultural settings. Many of these new relationships are built on respect or practical expediency and are free of both the binding intimacy of the culturally sanctioned vehicles and the conventional propriety once required of male-female interactions, which occurred outside these vehicles.

It remains to be seen, however, whether widespread sex integration will have an attenuating effect on marriage and family. The statistics on divorce would appear to give little comfort to those committed to marital permanence and family integrity and suggest that, on balance, the new sex integration may be incompatible with traditional institutions that place a high premium on exclusive personal loyalty. The new modes of cross-sex interaction tend to be *inclusive*, thereby coexisting poorly with modes, such as marriage, that make *exclusive* demands on men and women. Again, the basic questions must be raised: "Does the new degree of sex integration provoke an intolerable quantum of jealousy and strain in the average person who has one foot in tradition and the other in contemporary folkways? How well are people accommodating to knowing members of the opposite sex as friends and associates, not only as lovers, spouses, or relatives?" Asking the questions in this manner is not meant to prejudge the answers; it is only to recognize that basic changes do not occur without arousing basic doubts.

It might also be interesting to speculate in passing on the disruptive effect sex integration has had on same-sex "bonding" practices. It is increasingly rare and quite déclassé for heterosexual, middle class women and men to have outlets for association only with members of their own sex, as both sexes have invaded one another's formerly exclusive preserves. Again sex integration has rendered the traditional and exclusive forms of bonding outmoded. It is a matter of conjecture whether such bonding practices formerly served adaptive or superficial functions, but they were at one time very common in American society, particularly among men. Ironically, it is women who are reviving such practices in the form of sexually exclusive consciousness-raising groups, thus suggesting that bonding does have a purpose and that much of that purpose has been lost with the gradual loss of bonding.

I have already briefly alluded to the breakdown of the traditional double standard of sexual expression. Birth control technology, along with other changes in sexual attitudes, has conferred more sexual initiative to women. This has proliferated opportunities for sexual experience for both men and women, but it has also had the effect of placing pressure on the two sexes to perform sexually and to compartmentalize sexual *behavior* from affectionate and loving *feelings*. In contrast to earlier cultural expectations, women in particular are pressured to be sexually active and to abandon restraints, as the old stigma associated with being sexually expressive has been replaced by the converse stigma of being sexually inhibited. While, in one sense, many women may view this as a desirable hedonistic outcome and a refreshing departure from the Victorian legacy of repressed female sexuality, in another sense it is often felt as an infringement on their freedom of choice and action. Thus, the newly emerging "single standard" is in some respects as unsettling and anxiety producing as the old double standard was unfair and repressive.

From the male perspective, the response to female sexual initiative has run the gamut from acceptance to fear. Many men have welcomed the new initiative because it has freed them from the necessity of un-relenting sexual assertiveness and has allowed them to broaden their sexual repertoire to include more passive forms of expression. However, men may also resent the new female initiative because they view it as a usurpation of their own initiative and, in a broader sense, of their masculinity. Finally, liberated female sexuality has raised questions for many men about their own sexual adequacy. For some, the prospect and/or reality of being sexually outperformed by women constitutes a deep injury to their masculine narcissism and arouses basic fears about their adequacy as men.

Since the social status of men has been traditionally more valued than that of women, it is natural that men would respond more sus-piciously than women to alterations in status arrangements. In fact, many men have a pervasive sense of resentment as they see the social and economic gains of women as encroachments upon their own privi-leged status. While these apprehensions are real enough in a subjective sense, they correspond only partly with objective reality. In fact, we are not yet witnessing the dissolution of Western patriarchy, nor has there been any egregious diminution in the degree of male dominance in American society. At the lower and middle echelons of political, eco-nomic, and social control, men are sharing more of their functions with women than they have in the past, but there has been very little sharing at the top levels, and it is improbable that a woman will soon be presi-dent of the United States, General Motors, or The American Bar Associa-tion. Parenthetically, it is also improbable that ordinary men such as myself will soon occupy these positions. Thus, the symbolic dominance of the male sex promises to be a real factor in the lives of women *and* men for some time to come. Nevertheless, there is a process nibbling at the innards of the cultural vehicles that have traditionally brought men and women together, only to keep them apart—again I refer to courtship, marriage, family, and division of labor. They are all vastly dif-ferent, through several decades of erosion, from what they once were.

Let me also say that over the long run the average man may discover that there are basic human benefits in not having one's self-esteem dependent upon compulsive assertions of dominance, ambition, initiative, and the other ulcer-producing prerogatives of traditional masculinity. But these are the benefits of sex-role change that Selma Greenberg has so wisely suggested men have been taught to despise. Thus I am not sure that their widespread discovery is imminent, although I'd gladly have my skepticism disproved.

In summary, these many changes in the cultural fabric, primarily of middle class society but also in important respects in the cultural fabric of minority group societies as well, have had a double-edged effect on the psychological state of men and women. Viewed from one perspective, the changes have ushered in a new era of sex-role sensibility, one full of obvious promise for women and somewhat less obvious, although potentially great, benefit to men. But from another perspective, the changes have caused considerable psychological dislocation, leaving many with a split consciousness. They look nostalgically back at the old sex roles while simultaneously groping for new and relevant criteria of sex identity. The sexes continue to differ in significant ways, even while their common humanity makes them vastly more similar than different. However, it is no longer apparent to many people which differences and similarities are functional and which are not. When and if we are ever socialized to think that such considerations are not central to personal identity, they shall play a less central role in human psychology, in human culture, and in human survival.

In the meantime, we must get on with the business of reinventing sex roles so as to make them more congruent with the larger reinvention of our culture as a whole. The future of human society is crashing down on our heads. There is little doubt in my mind that the reinvention of sex role is central to our survival in the future—it is also clear to me that we are already in the future.

Let me end with a paraphrase of the modern American poet Theodore Roethke, who was also concerned with survival, both personal and cultural. In these two lines, Roethke (1961) spoke of the flow of water, but he may as well have been speaking of the flow of collected diversity. He said, quite simply:

(We) move as water moves . . .
Stayed by what was, and pulled by what would be.

REFERENCES

Parsons, T., and Bales, R. F. *Family, Socialization and Interaction Process.* New York: The Free Press, 1955.

Roethke, Theodore. *The Collected Verse of Theodore Roethke: Words for the Wind.* Bloomington: Indiana University Press, 1961, p. 153.

13

Epilogue

BARBARA SPRUNG
Director
Non-Sexist Child Development Project

S EVERAL activities related to furthering the goal of non-sexist early childhood education were undertaken as a direct result of the Conference on Non-Sexist Early Childhood Education.

Taking heed of suggestions made by conference participants, the staff of the Non-Sexist Child Development Project planned two major undertakings, which are described below:

Symposium on Multicultural Approaches to Non-Sexist Early Childhood Education

The Symposium was designed to bring together early childhood educators from many ethnic and cultural groups to discuss childrearing and educational practices. Five panelists representing a Native American, black, Asian American, Hispanic, and white ethnic perspective described childrearing within their group from a historical context, paying special attention to generational factors and differences in the social-ization of girls and boys. Following the panel, which provided the theo-retical background for the meeting, the participants heard a presenta-tion on collecting and evaluating multicultural materials for early child-hood classrooms and viewed a film on non-sexist curriculum taking place in multicultural pre-schools across the country.

These presentations provided practical suggestions for classroom use. The participants then went into small group sessions where they discussed the panel and materials/curriculum presentations from the perspective of their particular racial/ethnic group. The day ended with a report from each group, followed by interaction and a closing speaker who summarized the day's events.

The stated purpose of the Symposium was to provide a forum for discussion of the issue of how to achieve non-sexist programs in multi-cultural settings. This meeting was the first of its kind, and although con-crete suggestions did not emerge from the small group discussions, there was a strong feeling among the participants that the necessary first steps had been taken.

Insight was gained into the similarities in childrearing practices and cultural values among all the groups represented. While the need to eradicate sexism was acknowledged, it was not stated as a priority issue for several of the groups. The Non-Sexist Child Development Project expects to issue a report of the proceedings early in 1978 and to con-tinue to provide forums for further discussion of this issue.

A Training Model For Trainers

Acting directly on a suggestion made by Conference participants, the Project submitted a proposal to the USOE Women's Educational Equity Act to develop a training model and manual for Head Start Trainers. Since Head Start has a well established national training network with training offices in each of the ten HEW districts, it was felt that a program to offer non-sexist training within this network would have far reaching effects. The proposal was granted funds, and during 1978 the Project will cooperate with the training team in Region II to develop a model. After field testing the program throughout the region, which includes rural and urban populations, a manual for trainers will be written.

In 1979 the model and manual will be disseminated nationally, and support will be offered to help implement the program in other HEW regions. When completed the program will become available to teacher trainers within the largest existing early childhood education training network in the country. It is our hope that by training the trainers, who in turn train many thousands of teachers, who in turn interact with many more thousands of parents and children, we will integrate a non-sexist approach into the largest number of pre-school programs possible.

Other Developments

At the Conference early childhood researchers who are working in the area of sex role socialization realized that their work was not being disseminated fully enough to teachers and early childhood administrators who could translate their findings into program. They met together to plan strategies about how to remedy this. They decided to attend more teacher conferences (such as NAEYC, ACEI, and others) and report on their work.

Staff of the Non-Sexist Child Development Project also decided that we should include this information about new research in our workshops and lectures around the country. In this way an informal but essential network has begun and communication has been increased.

Again, responding to suggestions made at the Conference, the staff of the Project has prepared a comprehensive criteria for evaluating classroom materials and publications to ensure that they are non-sexist, nonracist, and of high educational quality. These Guidelines for the Development and Evaluation of Unbiased Educational Materials are given in the first appendix.

Appendices

Guidelines for the Development and Evaluation of Unbiased Educational Materials

FELICIA R. GEORGE
Trainer/Coordinator
Non-Sexist Child Development Project

D URING the National Conference on Non-Sexist Early Childhood Education, publishers of educational materials and professional journals met to define some strategies for implementing a non-sexist approach in materials for young children and their teachers. A majority of those who attended expressed the need for comprehensive guidelines to aid in the development and evaluation of materials that portray both sexes fairly and accurately while maintaining high standards of quality both in content and aesthetic appeal. There was a consensus that many of the earlier checklists were designed to deal with seemingly superficial facets of sexism, such as numbers of men and women and use of neuter or inclusive terms. In addition, they were anxious to help artists and publishers develop materials that would not sacrifice interesting story lines and attractive illustrations for sermons on equality or dull art work.

Since we know that materials can be non-sexist, appropriate, and appealing to young children and because we have a commitment to maintaining high standards in the development of such materials, the Non-Sexist

Child Development Project undertook the task of examining existing guidelines and refining them to reflect all the concerns expressed by members of the session on Educational Publishing. The focus of this checklist is to suggest ways of up-dating and improving the treatment of women and men in educational media. However, to be truly comprehensive the checklist must be revised periodically to deal with all forms of discrimination and to explore the issues of sexism and racism further. While the suggestions are directed toward the creators—writers and artists—many of the questions are also appropriate ones for publishers, teachers, parents, and readers. Later we hope to develop an even more comprehensive checklist addressed to all persons who create, evaluate, and use educational media for young children.

Due to publication deadlines, members who attended the session on Educational Publishing did not have an opportunity to give direct input into the creation of the guidelines that follow.

This checklist represents a compilation of existing materials,* many of which treat specific issues in greater depth. It would be beneficial for those who are considering particular aspects of the problem of fair representation to refer to the papers and publications cited in the references.

Introduction

These guidelines have been prepared by compiling information from the many evaluation forms and publishers' checklists that now exist. It does not cover every area in depth as an individual checklist may, but rather it deals generally with most of the issues related to eliminating sexism. The questions are taken from guidelines for print material, but many can be adapted for use in evaluating audio-visual media as well.

The guidelines have been divided into three sections—one refers specifically to visual stimuli (illustrations) and two apply to print or audio stimuli. The print-audio category has been further subdivided into the areas of content and language.

There are several points that need to be made about all aspects of a publication or media material in terms of unbiased portrayal of females and males. These considerations reflect our perspectives on quality materials.

1. The material should reflect an accurate and broad view of the world by presenting the various groups of people who make up this world.

---

* Sources are credited at the end. Because many of the guidelines cover the same points or overlap, individual items are not footnoted.

These groups may be determined by race, culture, ethnicity, age, physical and mental disability, class (economic status), creed, religion, and political ideology as well as sex. Material should depict the world as peopled equally by men and women in a variety of situations and show a balanced view of people in traditional and non-traditional roles. Moreover, material should reflect the changing nature of the world so that contemporary images as well as previously ignored historical figures and events are included.

Women and groups of people whose images have been left out of the materials for children need to be added as well. Finally, the portrayal of the world as the sole creation of white males must be corrected and enlarged by using information from other people's experiences and perspectives.

2. The emphasis should be on providing children with role models of competent humans who have a sense of self-worth and dignity. The characters should be people we want our children to emulate. They should display positive traits, such as the ability to solve problems, respect for others, concern for the well being of others, and physical and emotional strength. This is not to suggest that there should be no materials about social misfits or people who display traits considered to be anti-social, but rather that these issues should be very carefully treated in terms of helping children understand the full impact of these behaviors. Publishers and manufacturers need to be very careful about the definitions used to identify social deviance and failure.

The differences in treatment and opportunity afforded some groups need to be considered when developing stories about their condition in this society. Furthermore, care must be taken not to glorify attributes portrayed by famous national heroes that are otherwise considered socially unacceptable. Materials should help children identify the skills and characteristics that are beneficial to society as a whole and those that may only benefit individuals or select segments of society.

3. Materials should help children understand their real capabilities. Stories that emphasize unusual strength, magical powers, superhuman skill, or improbable solutions to problems do not help children grow or learn to use their own skills and strength. There needs to be room for some fantasy and imaginatively created worlds, but children are exposed through television and other media to a world in which solutions are worked out in the last few minutes of a program and enemies are dealt with by elimination.

Educational materials need to supply examples of problems that require work and time to solve and situations where adversaries coexist without destroying one another. It is especially important for young boys to understand that there are other important values beside being the super hero who always wins and who is always in control. Male children need to learn that they don't always have to have the answers or be in command so that they can begin to feel comfortable in calling on others, particularly females, to share responsibilities and solve problems.

4. Creators (writers and artists) need to be accurate in depicting physical images, life styles, cultural beliefs, and surroundings when portraying children from different racial and ethnic backgrounds. It is not enough to change skin color or names. Dialogue or story lines written for a white Anglo-Saxon child may be incorrect when used with images of black, Asian, or other children. Having materials prepared by creators of the same background as the characters in a story will go a long way toward ensuring cultural accuracy.

5. Girls and boys should be shown in cooperative action in both mixed and sex-segregated groupings. Materials that depict conflict and excessive competition do not promote a non-sexist attitude but rather create greater derisiveness and division between the sexes. Moreover, children need to be exposed to images of companionship and true friendship with members of the opposite sex, as well as with members of their own sex.

It is highly unlikely that all points on this checklist can be satisfied in an individual story or unit. However, within the total presentation of materials most of the suggestions can be included. Publishers and creators should aim for a balanced representation that includes males in roles traditionally considered "feminine" and females in roles traditionally considered "masculine" as well as females and males in traditional roles.

Illustrations

The illustrations in print material or visual stimuli in audio-visual media carry as important messages as the print or verbal content. Artists must be as conscious of standards for non-biased material as writers. Illustrations should complement the text and, when possible, assist in expanding the concepts presented. Visual clues should reflect the cultural values of the characters and accurately present the historical and social context of the story. As much care should be given to persons in the background (that is, illustrations of persons who are not main characters in the story) and animals as is given to the major protagonists.

—Do present a balanced number of males and females.

Crowd scenes should include a nearly equal number of males and females unless the story line clearly indicates that the situation calls for a predominantly male or female gathering. For example, a scene of the U.S. Senate would not include many female figures, and certainly the artist would not be expected to draw what doesn't exist. However, a scene of a medical convention can include a number of female figures and not be a sea of totally male faces.

—Do show non-traditional situations when possible to balance the number of traditional scenes drawn.

Where there is leeway the artist should take the opportunity to expand the child's view of the world. For example, if the text speaks only of a family scene, father may be shown washing dishes or feeding a baby instead of mother, or mother may be shown fixing a light switch or hanging pictures.

—Do picture women and men in numerous roles, both occupational and social.

Women and men should be pictured equally in every type of occupational and social role except those that are determined by sex, such as the role of father or mother, or that have been restricted historically, such as President of the United States or astronauts. The illustrator has an opportunity to include non-stereotyped images beyond what is indicated in the text. For example, the text may only speak of the teacher, principal, and school nurse without using either a pronoun or name. The illustrator has the option of drawing a young male teacher, a young female principal, and a older male nurse.

—Do show males and females working together in traditionally male and female activities.

Visual materials should show mixed sex groups playing together when the text does not specifically indicate that the group is homogeneous by sex. They should also include images of individual children working with items that have been classified for the opposite sex. For example, most schools still have boys' teams and girls' teams, but spontaneously formed teams on the local playground may consist of a few boys and girls. Boys may be shown cooking with girls or jumping rope.

—Do depict males and females as physically diverse.

Women and men come in all sizes and shapes. Their facial features also vary greatly, reflecting not only racial and ethnic differences but also variances of hair texture, skin type, and style. People have hair that varies from straight to curly, they are of diverse weight and height, some people wear glasses, some have beards and mustaches, and some are clean shaven. These varieties should be reflected.

—Do draw characters who are involved in heavy physical labor or dirty work appropriately dressed and portray the nature of the work accurately.

Persons shown doing heavy physical labor, such as scrubbing or ditch digging, should reflect the strength or effort needed to do the job, i.e., dirt on their work clothes, sweat on their brows, the strain of tense muscles. Thus a house cleaner pictured mopping the floor might have on comfortable work clothes and house shoes, and someone working in a garden might have soil on hands and coveralls.

—Do use a variety of illustrative styles and techniques to depict females and males.

To help break down former stereotyping, females can be drawn in bright primary colors using bold lines and males can be drawn in pastel colors with finer lines.

—Do include props, objects, and background settings that reflect non-stereotyped interests.

Although it may not be the focus of the text, the illustrator may wish to add background images that reflect culturally accurate non-sex stereotyped interests. For example, in a story where a girl is the main character, the artist might draw toy trucks or construction sets, along with dolls and tea sets, as part of her toy collection, or a boy may have a stuffed bear or needlework on his toy shelf.

—Do reflect an accurate historical and geographical view in the illustrations.

Scenes of contemporary urban, suburban, and rural life should reflect contemporary styles of dress and architecture. A scene of a city street should include women in pants and dresses and some men wearing flower-printed shirts or jewelry. A school scene should show girls and boys in pants and more casual dress. In addition, the class may have learning centers and open corridors instead of desks bolted down in a row. The number of women and girls in pants may vary depending upon the area that is represented as will style and type of dress. The same is true for males and boys drawn with longer hair.

Content

In addition to the story being told, the text of educational materials carries an important message about how females and males are viewed and valued. Be the main character female or male, be the plot involved with a tale of adventure or be it a reflective piece, there is much room within the work to present a positive, exciting image of both males and females. Creators must be conscious of what their creation brings to children both in its focal point and peripheral supporting information. It helps to consider the use of uncommon situations and non-traditional roles to bring a uniqueness and creativity to what otherwise might be just another story.

In evaluating the content of educational material, all the suggestions may not be applicable to a single story or unit. It is helpful to keep in mind that stereotyping does not occur in the portrayal of a specific incident or emotion but rather when there is an implication that this single incident reflects the norm or expected behavior or role for a particular group. Thus, objection is not made to showing a woman in the role of mother but to showing all and only women nurturers or implying that this role is the only role that a woman can fill. It is also unacceptable to indicate in any way that being a homemaker is less worthy or requires less skill than roles filled by other members of society.

To create material that is non-biased, we suggest that authors and creators of educational materials take care to address situations that are not usually presented and to do so in a way to suggest that, although the situation may not occur too frequently, it also is acceptable.

—Do prepare materials that call upon the creator's knowledge gained from having specific experiences or from being a member of a particular group.

The story of a Chinese-American girl's arrival in a new school is best told by a Chinese-American woman who has had that experience directly or who can draw upon her experiences in similar situations. This will insure that the perceptions unique to being a Chinese-American female will be presented and the plot will be embellished by non-stereotypical use of characters and events.

—Do present a balanced view of female and male images.

The leading characters of a piece should be females as often as they are males, and they should be portrayed in equally exciting roles. Males and females should be shown in plots involving action, adventure, strength, intelligence, sensitivity, perseverance, dreaming, decision making, contemplation, conflict, cooperation, and the like with the same frequency.

The female voice should be used as frequently as the male voice for narration.

—Do portray "traditional" female and male roles positively.

Traditional female roles have usually been depicted as inferior or less important or worthy than work or roles depicted for men. Those roles should be shown as valuable and important for both women and men. For example, the homemaker should be portrayed as someone who makes important decisions about essential purchases and provides for the emotional needs of the family members. Similarly, the image of the mischievous child should be recast to provide constructive solutions to problems caused by having a great deal of curiosity and activity.

—Do portray female and male characters in a variety of roles, situations, and conditions as unspectacular and expected occurrences.

Main and supporting characters should be depicted in a variety of nontypical but realistic roles. For example, in a story of a student who wins a science award, the main character might be a young girl with a female science teacher. The girl's mother might be a history professor who is pleased by her daughter's interest. Her classmates, both girls and boys, can be shown to have a variety of interests—from stamp collecting to needlepoint—and be pleased by her accomplishments. The story need not treat the girl as unusual because of her scientific ability.

Similarly there should be a balance of stories about girls who are physically active and competent and stories about boys who can prepare supper and look after young children. These activities may be included as only incidental to the plot.

—Do write about female and male characters who are individuals in their own right.

Female characters should be recognized for their own accomplishments and for their contributions to the plot. This is especially important when creating secondary or supporting characters. Good questions to ask of their roles are: "Who are the women and men in the story? What do they do? How does it influence or enhance the plot?"

They should be portrayed as having identifiable personalities and interests of their own. For example, a boy who runs home to tell his parents some good news might find mother varnishing the cabinet she's just completed or involved in work for the community center.

—Do portray all characters as having human attributes.

Both males and females should be shown as tender, strong, intelligent, witty, charming, competent, and so on, without deference to sex. The reader should be able to change the character's sex without drastically changing the integrity and coherence of the story. For example, a funny story should not become demeaning or insulting if the sex of the main character is reversed.

—Do write about all human conditions, including those that are not beautiful or popular.

Females and males can be found in a variety of situations. Creating positive materials does not prevent writers from picturing the diversity of human experiences. Women and men can have negative feelings or harmful attributes. They can be physically or mentally impaired. They live in all manner of social and economic conditions. A writer may need to exercise particular sensitivity when dealing with controversial issues or subjects that touch on feelings and thoughts that most people tend to avoid.

However, women and men who have physical disabilities do have rewarding experiences; people who have difficulty in supporting their physical needs for food and shelter have known joy; men and women who are not fiercely competitive have suceeded; and adding to one's material possessions is not everyone's goal.

—Do portray people as living in many types of family and community groupings.

Family means different things to different people depending on cultural background and/or experience. Some people share their household with others who are not related by blood; some live alone. Some children have had more than one set of grandparents or mothers and fathers by way of divorce and remarriage. Increasingly women are becoming the sole support of their children.

In addition, the various types of community groupings should be reflected. In urban areas apartment dwellers gather for tenant association meetings, families get together for block-sponsored activities, and groups organize around school-related functions. Community gatherings may differ somewhat in rural or suburban areas. Moreover, social groups are also formed on the basis of religion and other specialized interests.

—Do show males and females engaged in a variety of social, economic, and professional relationships.

The males and females that appear in materials for children may be husband/wife, classmates, friends, neighbors, business partners, professional associates, or others. Depicting a variety of adult relationships helps children understand social groupings and appropriate behaviors. For example, the grandmother in a story may have a close female friend with whom she shares her feelings and she may work with the man down the street on raising money for the town's health center. An older brother might belong to an association of real estate agents with his best friend, a woman.

—Do write about issues and experiences in a manner that makes them relevant to children's own experiences and knowledge.

Almost all, if not all, issues can be presented to children in a style and format that are comprehensible, appropriate, and tasteful. However, if the message of a story or presentation becomes too heavy and overshadows all else, the creator may lose the opportunity to reveal the moral or a new way of looking at life. The tone, the story, and the characters must all work together to hold interest and make the point.

Language

The language of a piece of work conveys meaning beyond the definition of individual words. Many words in the English language cause the reader/listener to picture men, even when a more inclusive image is meant. Moreover, occupational terms tend to depict the sex of the worker rather than describe the task being done.

Some changes can be made in the language that are fairly simple and tend to improve the accuracy of a description. Other changes may require rewriting or further thought about grammatical structure.

Since the changes that can be made in language are more concrete than those in the areas of illustrations and content, they have been clearly dealt with in several guidelines.* Grammatical convention and common usage may dictate the continued use of seemingly sexist phrases, such as words with masculine roots, i.e., mankind, and the generic "he," but the writer should be alert to possible alternatives and the thinking that suggests an advantage to using these alternatives.

—Do use terms that are neuter or truly inclusive of both sexes.

Many sentences can be rewritten in the plural form or passive voice or reworded to eliminate the gender pronoun to avoid using the generic "he." Use words such as consumer, when referring to someone making a purchase, instead of housewife. Use the terms listed in the *Revised Dictionary of Occupational Terms*, published by the Department of Labor, when referring to characters' careers or jobs. These terms do not denote the sex of the laborer and in most cases provide a more accurate description of the job. For example, fire fighter is a better indication of what the job entails than the sex-typed term fireman.

---

* See reference listing.

—Do use parallel language in speaking of men and women.

When describing or comparing men and women use a parallel reference. The emphasis should be on what is being compared; therefore, a woman's lineage or physical attributes are mentioned only when it is the focus of the comparison. For example, "Bob Smith, a well-known corporate lawyer, and Carol Mays, a famous entrepreneur," is acceptable, whereas "Bob Smith, a corporate lawyer, and Carol Mays, a vivacious blond," is not.

—Do refer to female characters by their own names and identities.

Although the woman in a story may be related to a main male character, she still has her own name and identity. For example, Martha Washington may have been George Washington's wife, but she had her own name and should be known for her accomplishments beyond those of her role as wife. Similarly the "farmer's wife" is undoubtedly part owner and laborer on the farm and should enjoy the title farmer.

—Do alternate the order of using female and male pronouns and nouns.

Placing boys or men first in every instance where both sexes are referred to implies that they are more valued or entitled to first consideration. Alternating the placement of gender related nouns and pronouns indicate that there is no specified position or order for women and men in this society.

We hope that these guidelines will serve as suggestions and examples of alternatives to what has traditionally been found in learning materials for children. They are by no means the last word on eliminating sex-role bias or other forms of discrimination but hopefully they will provide insights into how to deal with other concerns.

We hope that those responsible for the production of educational materials for young children will use these guidelines to assist them in creating products that are accurate, fair, and positive. And, we hope that those who work with young children will re-examine their teaching tools in light of the awareness and sensitivity that the guidelines provide.

Checklist Questions

* How many women and men are pictured in street or crowd scenes? How many older people? How many young adults or adolescents are pictured? How many babies?
* How many times is a woman drawn when the text calls for a police officer, carpenter, or shop owner when the sex is not indicated?

- How many times is a man drawn when the text calls for a nurse, clerk, or babysitter when the sex is not otherwise indicated?
- Is mother sometimes shown hammering in a workshop or fixing a leaky faucet in domestic scenes?
- Is father shown washing dishes or diapering a baby?
- How many females are shown as physically active? concentrating?
- How many males are shown as helping? watching?
- How many women are supervisors or in positions of authority?
- How many men are being supervised or directed by women?
- How many aging women and men are shown as active in family or community events?
- Do any mothers work outside the home? What do they do? What are fathers shown doing in the home?
- Is the person who takes care of the children when the parents aren't home always female?
- Is the participation of females or males in nontraditional activities always made the focal point of the story?
- Do the background or incidental props in the scene expand the readers' (viewers') knowledge and understanding of the characters and/or plot? Do they reveal non-stereotyped interests or culturally relevant values that are not necessarily specified in the story?
- In neighborhood scenes of the basketball court, marble match, or street stick ball game, are all participants always drawn as males? In scenes of jump rope, circle games, or doll house play, are all the participants always female?
- Are all men and boys always drawn as taller and heavier than women and girls?
- Are only small males (thin or short) depicted when the text indicates that the character is physically or emotionally weak? Are only large females drawn when the text indicates a physically or emotionally strong woman?
- Are big people always drawn when the text indicates physically strong or socially powerful males or females, i.e., is the football hero always a 250-pound 6-footer and the class valedictorian a slim, unathletic type?
- Are the leaders and stars always drawn larger than others? Are big people drawn as just one of the team?
- Are girls always depicted in pastel colors, drawn with fine, light lines? Are boys drawn in bright primary colors with bold lines?
- Can the character's sex be changed without changing the way the character is portrayed? Would the story be demeaning or silly if the pronoun he (she) were substituted for she (he)?
- Are all characters always attractive and skilled in all areas?
- Are people who lack material wealth shown as having valuable attributes? Do they express love for one another, joy, and pride in themselves?
- Are men and women shown who have won respect by helping others or appreciation by doing the "behind the scenes" tasks?

Guidelines for Evaluation of Materials • 165

- Are the rewards for a job well done sometimes inner satisfaction or admiration from the group?
- Is there always a mother and father in the families depicted?
- Are visiting grandparents, the natural mother's or father's parents? Does it make a difference?
- Is an aunt or uncle ever shown as being responsible for a child?
- Who are the important, influential adults in the story? Are they related in any way to the child? Are they counted as part of the child's family?
- Are the children always blood relations to the adults? Would including an adopted child change the story? How?
- How do the women and men interact?
- Are people—children and/or adults—ever described as being in close physical contact, i.e., holding hands, kissing, arm-in-arm?
- Do mixed age groups appear in the stories? How do the young and older members of the group relate to one another?
- Is the vocabulary at the child's level of comprehension?
- Is the major concept presented clearly and broken down into ideas that children can understand and relate to their own experiences?
- Does the material shock or invoke very strong emotions in the reader/viewer? Does this interfere with or enhance the intent of the story?
- Generally does this material add to the readers' (viewers') knowledge or understanding?
- What can a child learn from this material? About life? About women and men?
- Do the terms used to describe the females denote different attributes, status, or skills than those used to describe the males? Are women referred to as appendages or possessions of their husbands and/or fathers? Is the same respect given to males and females by use of parallel titles, names, and/or occupational terms?
- Can you describe the women in the story without making reference to a male counterpart, be it father, husband, or son?

REFERENCES

Association for Supervision and Curriculum Development. Resolution #8; Women and Minority Groups in Instructional Materials. Anaheim, CA., 1974.

Baltimore Feminist Project. *Sexism and Racism in Popular Basal Readers.* New York: Racism and Sexism Resource Center for Educators, 1976.

Britton, Gwyneth. *Textbook Analysis Kit for Sexism/Racism/Career Roles.* Corvallis: Gwyneth Britton & Associates. (Available from publisher, 1054 N.W. Fillmore, Corvallis, OR. 97330.)

California State Department of Education. *Guidelines for Evaluation of Instructional Materials for Compliance with Content Requirements for the Education Code.* Sacramento: 1976.

Committee on Classroom Practices in Teaching English: *Classroom Practices in Teaching English 1976-1977: Responses to Sexism.* Urbana: National Council of Teachers of English, 1976.

Committee on the Role and Image of Women in the Council and Profession of NCTE. *Guidelines for Combating Sexism in Language.* Urbana: National Council of Teachers of English, n.d.

. *Guidelines for Publication,* n.d.

. *Guidelines for Confronting Attitudes that Penalize Women,* n.d.

. *Guidelines for Nonsexist Use of Language in NCTE Publications,* n.d.

Feelings, Tom. *Remarks presented as a member of the selection committee and panelist for the Bias-Free Illustration Exhibit.* Exhibit co-sponsored by the American Institute of Graphic Arts, The Council on Interracial Books for Children, and the Textbook Committee of the New York Chapter of NOW. New York, December 13, 1976.

Feminists on Children's Media. *Little Miss Muffet Fights Back.* New York: 1979.

Guidelines on Choosing Toys for Children. New York: Public Action Coalition on Toys, n.d. (Available for $1.00 from PACT, c/o Vicki Reiss, 38 West 9th St., New York, NY 10011.)

Harper & Row. *Guidelines for Eliminating Stereotypes from Instructional Materials Grades K-12.* New York: 1978. (Available free April 1978, from publisher, School Department, 10 East 53rd Street, New York, NY 10022.)

Heilbroner, Robert L. *Don't Let Stereotypes Warp Your Judgement.* New York: Anti-Defamation League of B'nai B'rith, 1971.

Holt, Rinehart and Winston. *Guidelines for the Development of Elementary and Secondary Instructional Materials: The Treatment of Sex Roles.* New York: 1975. (Available free from publisher, School Department, 383 Madison Avenue, New York, NY 10017.)

Kalamazoo Public Schools. *Guidelines for the Evaluation of Print and Non-Print Materials.* Kalamazoo, MI: Instructional Media Department, 1973.

J.B. Lippincott Company. *Guidelines to Promote the Awareness of Human Potential.* Philadelphia: n.d. (Available free from publisher, East Washington Sq., Philadelphia, PA 19105.)

McGraw-Hill Book Company. *Guidelines for Equal Treatment of the Sexes in McGraw-Hill Book Company Publications.* New York: n.d. (Available free from publisher, 1221 Avenue of the Americas, New York, NY 10020.)

Macmillan Inc. *Guidelines for Creating Positive Sexual and Racial Images in Educational Materials.* New York: 1975. (Available free from publisher, 866 Third Ave., New York, NY 10022.)

Michigan Women's Commission. *Sex Discrimination in an Elementary Reading Program: A Report Based on the Work of the Committee to Study Sex Discrimination in the Kalamazoo Public Schools.* Lansing:, n.d.

Guidelines for Evaluation of Materials • **167**

Moberg, Verne. *A Child's Right to Equal Reading: Exercises in the Liberation of Children's Books from the Limitations of Sexual Stereotypes.* Washington, D.C.: National Education Association, n.d.

National Education Association. *How Fair Are Your Children's Textbooks?* Washington, D.C.: n.d. (Available from Publications Order Dept., Academic Building, Saw Mill Road, West Haven, CT 06516.)

New York State Education Department: *Reviewing Curriculum for Sexism.* Albany: 1975.

Nilsen, Allen Pace, et al. *Sexism and Language.* Urbana: National Council of Teachers of English, 1977.

Racism and Sexism Resource Center for Educators. *Stereotypes, Distortions and Omissions in U.S. History Textbooks.* New York: 1977.

————. *Ten Quick Ways to Analyze Children's Books for Racism and Sexism,* 1974. (Available from the Council on Interracial Books for Children, 1841 Broadway, New York, NY 10023.)

Science Research Associates, Inc. *Fairness in Educational Materials: Exploring the Issues.* Chicago: 1976. (Available free from publisher, 259 East Erie St., Chicago, IL 60611.)

Scott, Foresman and Company. *Guidelines for Improving the Images of Women in Textbooks.* Glenview: 1974. (Available free from publisher, 1900 East Lake Ave., Glenview, IL 60025.)

Weitzman, Lenore J. et al. *Sex-Role Socialization in Picture Books for Preschool Children.* Pittsburgh: KNOW, Inc., 1972.

Wilson, Geraldine L. *A Classroom Survey of Literature for Children.* New York: New York City Head Start Regional Training Office, May 1976.

————. *Curriculum Development and Planning: Imperatives for a Just Curriculum.* Paper presented at A Symposium on Multicultural Approaches to Non-Sexist Early Childhood Education (sponsored by the Non-Sexist Child Development Project of the Women's Action Alliance, Inc.) November 4, 1977, at New York University.

————. and Rosner, Sophie P. *Some Criteria for the Selection of Picture Books for Children.* New York: New York City Head Start Regional Training Office, May 1976.

Women on Words and Images. *Dick and Jane as Victims: Sex Stereotyping in Children's Readers,* expanded 1975 edition. Princeton, NJ: 1975.

————. *Help Wanted: Sexism in Career Education Materials.* Princeton, NJ: 1975.

Sources of
Non-Sexist Materials

Films

Campus Film Distributors Corp.
2 Overhill Road
Scarsdale, NY 10583

SOUTHERN BLACK CHILDREN, Part II. (from the "Play and Cultural Continuity" series). Shows scenes of black children from the South in various child care settings. Provides stimulus for discussion on differences in the play of boys and girls in these various settings. Of the four films in the series, this one was reviewed. We strongly urge interested persons to carefully preview the other three films. (27 mins., color, 1975, teacher training)

Contemporary/McGraw-Hill
Film Preview Library
P.O. Box 590
Hightstown, NJ 08520

FREE TO BE YOU AND ME. A film of the TV Special. Available as one 40-minute film or three 14-minute segments. For sale or rental. (color, 1974, classroom grade 3 +)

SEX ROLE DEVELOPMENT. Gives an overview of the ways sex-role stereotypes are perpetuated and shows how one set of parents and a pre-school program are trying to provide children with alternatives. (22 mins., color, 1974, teacher training, parent education)

Extension Media Center
University of California
Department SR-1
Berkeley, CA 94720

ANYTHING THEY WANT TO BE. Vignettes of classroom scenes illustrating how girls are discouraged from succeeding in intellectual and career-oriented tasks. (7 mins., color, 1974, classroom grade 3+, teacher training)

CHANGING IMAGES—CONFRONTING CAREER STEREOTYPES. Shows

third- and fourth-graders at work as they challenge career stereotyping. Children discuss football players, nurses, family activities, etc. For sale or rental. (16 mins., black and white, 1975, grade 3+, teacher training)

HEY! WHAT ABOUT US? Illustrates sex-role stereotyping of physical activities in elementary school settings. (15 mins., color, 1974, grade 3+, teacher training)

I IS FOR IMPORTANT. Focuses on sex-role stereotyping in social interaction and emotional expression. Situations involve children from grades K through 8. (12 mins., color, 1974, grade 3+, teacher training)

Mass Media Ministries
2116 No. Charles St.
Baltimore, MD 21218

TV—THE ANONYMOUS TEACHER. Interview with a psychologist on the effects of television is punctuated with film clips of young children watching T.V. The narrator comments on effects of television on children's attitudes and behavior, violence, commercial advertising, sex-role and racial stereotyping, and child viewing of adult programs, among other issues. Produced by United Methodist Communication (15 mins., color, 1976, teacher training, parent education)

New Day Films
P.O. Box 315
Franklin Lakes, NJ 07417

THE FLASHETTES. A moving film about a girls' track team that illustrates the value of sports in developing self-confidence and a cooperative spirit. Sensitively shows the joy and pain of competition. Directed by Bonnie Friedman. (20 mins., color, 1976, grades 3-6, teacher training).

Non-Sexist Child Development Project
370 Lexington Avenue, Room 2215
New York, NY 10017

THE SOONER THE BETTER: Non-Sexist Education for Young Children. Depicts non-sexist preschool classroom practices. Shot on location in schools from Boston to San Diego, it has a truly multiracial tone. Excellent for pre-service and in-service teacher training programs and for parent education courses at the high school level. A study guide and classroom checklist hand-out provide material for in-depth discussion of the points illustrated. (Available for purchase or rental, 27 mins., color, 1977, teacher training; distributed by Third Eye Films, 12 Arrow St., Cambridge, MA 02138)

THE TIME HAS COME: An Approach to Non-Sexist Parenting. A complementary film to *The Sooner the Better*. This film is designed for parents and depicts and discusses non-sexist child rearing. Also filmed on location in cities from Boston to San Diego, it too is multiracial and has a soft approach and encouraging tone. Suitable for parent discussion groups and as a teacher training aid in how to work with parents. Also useful for parent education programs at the high school level. (23 mins., color, 1977, parent education, teacher training)

ODEON Films, Inc.
1619 Broadway
New York, NY 10019
SUGAR AND SPICE. Shows what is being done in three schools in New York and Massachusetts to eliminate sex-role stereotyping. Focuses on changes in curriculum, teacher attitude, and parent awareness. Produced in cooperation with the Women's Action Alliance, Inc. Available for purchase or rental with accompanying study guide and resource list (32 mins., color, 1974, teacher training).

Phoenix Films, Inc.
470 Park Avenue South
New York, NY 10016
GIRLS SPORTS: On the Right Track. Summarizes recent changes in sports for girls. Using track and field events as an example, portrays historical overview of women's achievements in these sports and the limitations and barriers they need to overcome. The experiences of three high school girls show the new opportunities available for girls today. (17 mins., color, 1976, junior high school, training for physical education teachers)

Filmstrips

Scholastic Magazines, Inc.
Audio Visual Dept.
50 W. 44th Street
New York, NY 10036
BEGINNING CONCEPTS—PEOPLE WHO WORK. Ten sound/color filmstrips with cassettes or records depicting men and women at work at their unusual, nontraditional careers, 1975.
FIVE CHILDREN and FIVE FAMILIES. A cultural awareness sound/color filmstrip program. While not specifically designed as non-sexist materials, the filmstrips are unusually sensitive portrayals of a wide variety of family lifestyles. *Five Families* is about life in a Chinese, Native American, Mexican American, black, and white family. *Five Children* shows how children live in various geographic locations. Available in Spanish and English.
EXPLORE. A set of 3 units each containing 4 sound/color filmstrips, student logbooks, and teaching guide. Units are designed to aid children in defining work and play. They discuss how an individual's personality and interests influence career choices and explore several careers. The actual voices of the

men, women, girls, and boys featured in the filmstrips were taped and provide a very real touch. The program was designed with 4-6 graders in mind, but some of the filmstrips are certainly useful for grades 7-8 as well.

Slide Shows

Educational Alliance Day Care Center
197 East Broadway
New York, NY 10002

A NON-SEXIST CURRICULUM FOR EARLY CHILDHOOD. A slide presentation of the Non-Sexist Child Development Project as it developed at the Educational Alliance Day Care Center. Ann-Marie Mott and Sally Smith have turned their pictorial anecdotal records of what happens when teachers introduce children to non-sexist curriculum into an inspiring audio-visual account. (20 mins., available with cassette or script in 1976). Also available as a filmstrip with sound.

Resource Center on Sex-Role in Education
1201 16th St., N.W., Rm. 701
Washington, DC 20036

IMAGES OF MALES AND FEMALES IN ELEMENTARY SCHOOL TEXTBOOKS. Documents differential treatment of males and females in math, science, reading, and social studies texts, grades 1-6. Comes with booklet summarizing findings of the study and suggesting actions to be taken by teachers, administrators, parents, and students. (Booklet can be ordered in bulk; 45 mins., with synchronized cassette tape and script, 1974).

Women on Words and Images
Box 2163
Princeton, NJ 08540

DICK AND JANE AS VICTIMS: Sex-Role Stereotyping in Children's Readers. Results of a research project on sexism in children's reading texts presented in dramatic visual form. Images of the way readers represent the stereotyped role of young and adult males and females. A booklet by the same title provides the rationale, procedure, and findings of the study. (30 mins., with synchronized cassette tape and script, 1976 revised expanded edition).

HELP WANTED. A slide presentation on sexism in career materials similar in scope and impact to the *Dick and Jane* slides. Booklet also available. (25 mins., with synchronized cassette tape and script, 1975).

SEXISM IN FOREIGN LANGUAGE TEXTBOOKS. A presentation on sexism in foreign language texts. (25 mins., with synchronized cassette tape and script, 1975).

Records

Caedmon Records
505 Eighth Avenue
New York, NY 10018
HURRAY FOR CAPTAIN JANE, 1975. Non-sexist stories by Tammy Grimes. (Other titles for older children also available.)

Free to Be Foundation
370 Lexington Avenue
Room 412, Dept. LW
New York, NY 10017
FREE TO BE YOU AND ME - by Bell Records. A project of the Ms. Foundation. (Also available at record shops.)

Photographs and Posters

Change for Children
532 Valencia St.
San Francisco, CA 94110
PEOPLE AT WORK PHOTO PACKET. A packet of 20 8" x 10" black and white photos of women and men in various non-traditional jobs.
WOMEN AT WORK. A packet of 15 8" x 10" photo reproductions of women of different ages and ethnic backgrounds working in non-traditional jobs.

David C. Cook Publishing Co.
School Products Division
Elgin, IL 60120
THE AMERICAN WOMEN'S ROLE - Yesterday and Today. A set of 16 12" x 17" color pictures with accompanying 32-page manual. Dramatizes past achievements of American women and focuses on opportunities for women's total involvement in America's future. Recommended for grades 4-8.

Exploring Childhood Program
Educational Development Center
15 Mifflin Pl.
Cambridge, MA 02138
WE ARE A FAMILY. A poster of many types of non-nuclear, multiracial, multiethnic families.

F.R.E.E. (Feminists for Equal Education)
Box 185
Saxonville Station
Framingham, MA 01701

RESOURCE PHOTOS OF WOMEN IN COMMUNITY JOBS. A set of eight 8"
x 10" black and white photos. Especially good because it depicts clearly rec-
ognizable community jobs such as a milk deliverer, a letter carrier, a police
officer, and a bus driver.

RESOURCE PHOTOS OF WOMEN IN PROFESSIONAL ROLES. Similar to the
Resource Photos of Women in Community Jobs with eight 8" x 10" black
and white photos. This set is not quite as good because some of the professions are a bit hard to define, i.e., a politician and a computer program-
mer, but others such as a judge and a potter are fine. Both sets are inex-
pensive and are a valuable resource.

Instructo   Corporation
Paoli, PA 19301

HOME AND FAMILY. Twenty-four pictures of family members in a variety of
situations. Includes images of family members of various ages and from different racial groups. Men are shown interacting with children in a nurturing
manner.

Scott, Foresman and Company
99 Bauer Dr.
Oakland, NJ 07436

MOTHERS DO MANY KINDS OF WORK. Poster of women engaged in several work situations. Free.

Women in Sports
c/o Pat Keuss and Cathy Cade
2103 Emerson St.
Berkeley, CA 94705

WOMEN IN SPORTS. A set of six 8½" x 10½" black and white photos depicting women and girls engaged in active sports. Shots include a weight lifter,
a gymnast, a javelin thrower, a batter, two judo experts, and sprinters.

Women's Action Alliance, Inc.
Non-Sexist Child Development Project
370 Lexington Avenue
New York, NY 10017

PEOPLE AT WORK. This set consists of 24 8" x 10" black and white photos of
people at work. Men and women have been photographed on location
doing their jobs. An effort has been made to find as many non-stereotyped
workers as possible. Produced by the Instructo Corporation.

RESOURCE PHOTOS OF MEN IN THE NURTURING ROLE. This set consists of eight 8" x 10" black and white photos of men interacting with young children. There are fathers, grandfathers, and men who work with children as teachers and pediatric nurses. Also included is a poster featuring a grandfather and granddaughter in a group of sequential photographs involving playing with grandpa's hat. This poster is ideally suited to a variety of language arts activities. Photographs by Jim Levine.

Puzzles and Dolls

Childcraft
20 Kilmer Road
Edison, NJ 08817
BODIES. A sturdy plywood-backed 25-piece puzzle made from an appealing color photo of a nude white male and a black female child. Can be used to illustrate accurately the real difference between males and females and to initiate discussion about the body. (Also, watch for non-sexist wooden puzzles designed by the Women's Action Alliance, Inc. for Childcraft.)
ETHNIC DOLLS. Asian-American Child - 26" long - boy only; Native-American Child - 18" long - girl only; Black Child - 18" long - available in girl and boy versions.
CLOTH DOLLS. Filled with polyurethane stuffing. Features are painted on; yarn hair and beaded eyes firmly fixed. Come dressed in overalls and T-shirts. Good huggable dolls made to withstand rough handling or loving.

Fisher of America, Inc.
Montclair, NJ 07042
CALEB. A black boy doll dressed like the typical four- or five-year-old at play. Not anatomically correct but at least he's an adequate role model for little boys. (Part of the Sasha Line.)

Mattel
2 Penn Plaza
New York, NY 10001
BABY BROTHER TENDER LOVE. An anatomically complete male doll available in black and white versions. A soft cuddly doll that will encourage nurturing play. Its realistic representation of the male body will ease anxieties raised in young boys upon seeing "incomplete" boy baby dolls.

Judy Puzzles
250 James Street
Morristown, NJ 07960
OCCUPATIONAL SERIES. Thirteen wooden puzzles depicting women in a

variety of roles, including some which are non-traditional. Puzzle series contains both black and white figures.

THE CITY. A 2' x 3' heavy plastic coated cardboard puzzle consisting of 20 pieces. Depicts a big city scene with people working and going about their daily chores. Puzzle shows images of black and white people and some women in nontraditional jobs.

THE PARK. Similar in size, material, and difficulty to *The City* puzzle except this item shows black and white people in a park setting. Includes a woman selling balloons and men caring for young children.

SAFETY. A 2' x 3' heavy plastic coated cardboard puzzle consiting of 15 pieces. Depicts street scene emphasizing steps to health and safety such as crossing at the crosswalks and discarding litter in trash basket. A poster of the same scene is also available on 2' x 3' plastic coated paper.

THE DOCTOR. Similar in size, material, and difficulty to *Safety* puzzle. Depicts scene in a medical center. Also available in poster version.

Games and Instructional Aids

Fundamentals
P.O. Box 263
South Pasadena, CA 91030

ROBOT. A non-sexist version of the "Old Maid" card game. The cards depict women and men in counterpart work roles and clothing.

Women's Action Alliance, Inc.
Non-Sexist Child Development Project
370 Lexington Avenue, Room 2215
New York, NY 10017

COMMUNITY CAREERS. Twenty-seven multiethnic figures of men and women dressed in clothing appropriate to their jobs. Flannelboard. Also contains interchangeable props and accessories relevant to the various community jobs and reading words that are non-sexist such as "repair person." Produced by Instructo Corporation.

MY FAMILY PLAY PEOPLE. Black and white family groups of block accessories contain two parent-age people, two older people, one teenager, and one small child. Allows children to reflect their own family reality rather than confining them to the nuclear or single ethnic family normally found in children's materials. Heavy cardboard, full-color back and front views with plastic stands. Produced by Milton Bradley.

OUR COMMUNITY HELPERS PLAY PEOPLE. Male and female letter carriers, construction workers, doctors, nurses, police officers, and business executives. Heavy cardboard, full-color back and front views with plastic stands. Produced by Milton Bradley.

PLAY SCENES LOTTO. A photographic color lotto depicting both girls and boys in active play. Contains four playing boards with six photos on each, plus matching cards. Multiracial and non-sexist. Produced by Milton Bradley.

Curriculum Programs

Program Department
Girl Scouts of the U.S.A.
830 Third Avenue
New York, NY 10022

FROM DREAMS TO REALITY: A Career Awareness Exploration Project. An excellent program of career education activities for young girls that includes packets on five areas of the world of work covering careers in health, arts-communication, science-business-technology, social-personal services, and careers out-of-doors. Each packet includes a set of career cards and a booklet of activities. The career cards describe representative jobs and present information about the type of work required through interview of an actual woman on the job. The booklets contain outlines for activities that help students discover their own interests and skills; activities that provide information about representative jobs as well as some that help young girls gain a realistic understanding of the effect working will have on their other possible roles (i.e., as student, wife, mother, single woman, etc.), and resources for gathering more information. There is an attempt to include women from different racial and ethnic backgrounds on the career cards. This program was designed for Cadettes and Senior Scouts and is suitable for ages 12-16. Some activities can be modified for younger children.

Project Equality
DL & Associates
29638 41st Place South
Auburn, WA 98002

A set of non-sexist career education materials that include: outlines of lesson plans for task simulation activities; pictures of job situations; outlines of lessons in career education; filmstrip-cassette presentation on selected occupations; a directory of speakers on careers (from the Washington area only); a resource list; and media display kits. For more detailed description and prices, write for an order form and free potpourri.

Women's Studies Program Office
Berkeley Unified School District
1720 Oregon Street
Berkeley, CA 94703

THE HOUSE THAT JILL AND JACK BUILT. A manual of instructions for equipping and buying supplies for a carpentry program. Contains outlines of carpentry lessons and non-sexist stories, which, when combined, form a unit to develop a non-sexist introduction to carpentry as a career. The manual also includes a list of supplementary resources and pictures of children involved in carpentry work.

Reading Texts

The publishers of the following basal reading series have made a serious attempt to fairly represent both sexes and the various cultural and ethnic groups that comprise American society. Although other publishers whose names do not appear on this list have made similar efforts, we have listed these particular series because of their sensitivity in addressing the issues of racial and sex-role discrimination and for the quality of production in both literary and illustrative style.

Harper & Row
10 East 53rd Street
New York, NY 10022

READING BASICS PLUS, 1976. A series of three reading readiness books: *Get Ready*, *Get Set*, and *Go Read*; three pre-primers: *Places and Puzzles*, *Rain and Riddles*, *Fish and Fables*; a primer, *Webs and Wheels*; and a first reader, *Socks and Secrets*.

Readiness books are attractively colorful workbooks with a combination of realistically drawn and cartoon-like figures that reflect contemporary styles. The other books—soft-covered pre-primers, and hard-covered primers and reader—use a combination of colorful drawings and photographs. Stories are interspersed with other types of language arts activities.

D.C. Heath Canada Ltd.
100 Adelaide St., W.
Suite 1408
Toronto, Ontario

WOMEN AT WORK, 1975. The stories of eight women and their nontraditional activities presented in individual paperback books using color photos taken of the women at work. A sample of the activities and occupations shown are fish dealer, pilot, house builder, veterinarian, and television producer. The one drawback is that there is no racial diversity among the group of women featured. However, in this case the series is about actual women in Western Canada and accurately reflects the population.

Houghton Mifflin Company
One Beacon St.
Boston, MA 02107

The primers and early readers of the Houghton Mifflin Reading Series reviewed include the following: *Rockets, Surprises, Footprints, Honeycomb, Cloverleaf, Sunburst, Tapestry, Windchimes,* and *Passports.*

The first three books are soft-covered primers illustrated with a combination of cartoon-like and realistic drawings. The more difficult readers use a combination of children's stories written by well-known authors, traditional stories found in readers, poems, skill lessons, and plays. In the most advanced readers, stories written by well-known children's authors are used exclusively, and photographs are introduced as illustrations.

Scott, Foresman and Company
1900 East Lake Avenue
Glenview, IL 60025

Scott, Foresman and Company has come a long way from its early Dick, Jane, and Sally readers and should be commended.

READING UNLIMITED, revised levels 1-21, is for elementary grades.

Something Special (Kindergarten Program). Truly "something special." A soft-covered workbook, which includes brightly colored drawings and photographs. Some of the pictures are taken from familiar picture books. The racial mix is the best seen to date, and both boys and girls are shown in a variety of active and passive activities.

Reading Unlimited (Levels 1-4, grade 1). A set of 31 soft-covered early readers. The level 1 books have only bright, clear photographs and drawings for object identification and picture reading. Text is introduced in the last book. The illustrative style for books at all levels include drawings and photographs. A combination of well-known children's stories and traditional basal reader stories are used throughout. Levels 3 and 4 include stories to develop direction-following skills and concept building. There is a good ethnic mix throughout these books.

Get Set (Kindergarten - grade 1). The first book of the reading series. A soft-covered book with bright drawings and photographs. Introduces vocabulary and simple sentences.

Ready to Roll (primer level); *Rolling Along* (book 1, part 2); *More Power* (book 2, part 1); *Moving Ahead* (book 2, part 2). These hard-covered books follow the same format as books in the other Scott, Foresman series.

All series are accompanied by excellent teaching editions with added features of suggestions on how teachers can adapt reading programs to children with learning disabilities, to children who are bilingual, and to children with other special needs. Also has a section on involving families in the learning process.

Guidelines

Several publishers and educational groups offer guidelines for avoiding sexist language and concepts in textbooks and other curriculum materials. See the References at the end of the Guidelines for the Development and Evaluation of Unbiased Educational Materials in the preceding appendix for a listing.

Books and Toy Distributors

Academy Press Limited
370 No. Michigan Avenue
Chicago, IL 60601

A publishing company that has printed several publications on non-sexist education. Of special note, *The Liberty Cap: A Catalog of Non-Sexist Materials for Children* by Enid Davis is a directory of more than 1,000 book, record, and film reviews. Also, contact Enid Davis, 1050 Newell Road, Palo Alto, CA. 94303, for back issues of the newsletter from which this directory was compiled.

Child's Play
226 Atlantic Avenue
Brooklyn, NY 11201

One of the best collections of non-sexist children's books to be found. It sells mail order and has a catalog.

Gryphon House
P.O. Box 274
Mt. Rainer, MD 20822

It distributes an excellent collection of high-quality children's books, many with non-sexist and multiracial titles. The new catalog has an author-title index and a subject area index. Under the subject area index are subheadings of books on topics such as handicapped children, black children, girls, single-parent families, adoption, etc.

Learn Me, Inc.
642 Grand Ave.
St. Paul, MN 55105

It carries all kinds of high-quality educational materials that have been screened for sexism and racism in addition to non-sexist, multiracial books. Write for catalog to order by mail.

The Open Book
1025 Second Avenue
Salt Lake City, UT 84103
A bookstore specializing in non-sexist books for children as well as women's books.

Toys That Care and Other Items, Inc.
P.O. Box 81
Briarcliff Manor, NY 10510
A distributor of educational materials. It also offers consultation services.

Feminist Publishers

The Feminist Press
Box 334, SUNY
Old Westbury, NY 11568
Non-sexist books, bibliographies, resource booklets, curriculum materials, and the like. Excellent resources for elementary, high school, and adult feminist materials. Especially useful is its recently revised publication, *Feminist Resources for Schools and Colleges: A Guide to Curricular Materials* by Merle Froschl and Jane Williamson.

Lollipop Power
P.O. Box 1171
Chapel Hill, NC 27514
Publishers and distributors of low-cost, non-sexist paperback picture books. Many excellent titles. Write for listing.

Resource Centers

Change for Children
532 Valencia St.
San Francisco, CA 94110
Workshops, courses, materials, bibliography of children's books, and consultation—all aimed at early childhood/elementary grade levels.

Far West Laboratories for Educational
 Research And Development
1855 Folsom St.
San Francisco, CA 94103
Workshops, consultations, films, curriculum information.

Resource Center on Sex Roles in Education
National Foundation for the Improvement
of Education
1201 16th St., N.W. - Rm. 701
Washington, DC 20036

A national center for the dissemination of information on non-sexist education, K-12.

Women's Action Alliance, Inc.
Non-Sexist Child Development Project, Room 2215
370 Lexington Avenue
New York, NY 10017

A national clearinghouse on non-sexist early childhood education offering workshops, consultation, curriculum development, non-sexist, multiracial materials, and information.

Suggested Reading

Aldous, Joan. "Children's Perceptions of Adult Role Assignment: Father Absence, Class, Race and Sex Influence." *Journal of Marriage and the Family*, Vol. 34, No. 1, February 1972, pp. 55-65.

American Association of Colleges for Teacher Education. "The Molding of the Non-Sexist Teacher." *Journal of Teacher Education*, Vol. XXVI, No. 4, Winter 1975.

American Association of School Administrators. *Sex Equality in Educational Materials*, "Executive Handbook" series, No. 4. Arlington, VA: 1975.

Angrist, Shirley. "The Study of Sex Roles." *Journal of Social Issues*, Vol. 1, 1969, pp. 215-232.

Bardwick, J.M. *Psychology of Women: A Study of Bio-Cultural Conflicts*. New York: Harper & Row, 1971.

———, and Douvan, Elizabeth. "Ambivalence: The Socialization of Women" in *Women in Sexist Society*, Gornick and Moran, eds. New York: Basic Books, pp. 147-159.

Bean, Joan P., and Kaplan, Alexandra G., eds. *Beyond Sex-Role Stereotypes: Readings Toward a Psychology of Androgyny*. Boston: Little Brown, 1976.

Bem, Daryl J., and Sandra L. "Training the Woman to Know Her Place" in *Sexism & Youth*, Diane Gersoni-Stann, ed. New York: R.R. Bowker Company, 1974.

Biller, H.B. *Father, Child and Sex Role*. Lexington, MA: D.C. Heath, 1971.

Breitbart, Vicki. *The Day Care Book*. New York: Alfred A. Knopf, 1974.

Broverman, I., et al. "Sex-role Stereotypes and Clinical Judgements of Mental Health." *Journal of Consulting Psychology*, Vol. 34, 1970, pp. 1-7.

Claven, S. "Women's Liberation and the Family." *Family Coordinator*, Vol. 19, 1970, pp. 317-323.

Cohen, Monroe, ed. *Growing Free. Ways to Help Children Overcome Sex-Role Stereotypes*. Washington, D.C.: Association for Childhood Educational International, 1976.

Courtney, A.E., and Lockeritz, S.W. "A Woman's Place: An Analysis of the Roles Portrayed by Women in Magazine Advertisements." *Journal of Marketing Research*, Vol. 8, 1971, pp. 92-95.

Cuffaro, H.K. "Psychological Theory and Child Development Background" and "Blocks," in *Guide to Non-Sexist Early Childhood Education*, B. Sprung, ed., New York: Women's Action Alliance, 1974.

Davis, Enid. *The Liberty Cap: A Catalog of Non-Sexist Materials for Children*. Chicago: Academy Press, 1977.

"The Ecology of Education: The American Family." *National Elementary Principal*, Part 1, Vol. 55, No. 5, May/June, 1976; Part 2, Vol. 55, No. 6, July/August 1976.

Eliasberg, Ann. "Are You Hurting Your Daughter Without Knowing It?" *Family Circle*, February 1971.

Epstein, R., and Liverant, S. "Verbal Conditioning and Sex-Role Identification in Children." *Child Development*, Vol. 34, 1963, pp. 99-106.

Ernest, John. *Mathematics and Sex*. Mathematics Department, University of California at Santa Barbara, January 1975.

Fagot, B.I., and Patterson, G. "An in Vivo Analysis of Reinforcing Contingencies for Sex-role Behaviours in the Preschool Child." *Developmental Psychology*, Vol. 1, 1969, pp. 563-568.

Federbush, Marcia. *Let Them Aspire: A Plea and Proposal for Equality of Opportunity for Males and Females in the Ann Arbor Public Schools*. Pittsburgh: KNOW, Inc., 1971.

Feminists on Children's Media. "A Feminist Look at Children's Books." *School Library Journal*, Vol. 18, 1971, pp. 19-24.

Frazier, Nancy, and Sadker, Myra. *Sexism in School and Society*. New York: Harper & Row, 1973.

Freeman, Jo. *The Building of the Gilded Cage*. Pittsburgh: KNOW, Inc. 1973.

Froschl, Merle, and Williamson, Jane. *Feminist Resource for Schools and Colleges*, rev. ed. Old Westbury, NY: The Feminist Press, 1977.

Gersoni-Stann, Diane. *Sexism and Youth*. New York: R.R. Bowker Company, 1974.

Golden, Gloria, and Hunter, Lisa. *In All Fairness: A Handbook on Sex Role Bias in Schools*. San Francisco: Far West Laboratory for Educational Research and Development, 1974.

Guttentag, Marcia, and Bray, Helen. *Undoing Sex Stereotypes: Research and Resources for Educators*. New York: McGraw-Hill, 1976.

Harrison, Barbara G. *Unlearning the Lie*. New York: Liveright, 1973.

Harrison, Linda. "Cro-Magnon Woman—in Eclipse." *The Science Teacher*, Vol. 42, No. 4, 1975, pp. 4-11.

Hartley, Ruth E. "Sex Role Pressures and the Socialization of the Male Child." *Psychological Reports*, 1959, pp. 457-68 (Also in *And Jill Came Tumbling After*).

Heatherington, E.M. "A Developmental Study of the Effects of Sex of the Dominant Parent on Sex-Role Preference, Identification, and Imitation on Children." *Journal of Personality and Social Psychology*, Vol. 2, 1965, pp. 188-194.

Holton, Susan. *Louisiana Women and Girls in Public Vocational-Technical Education Programs: A Study of Sex Discrimination*. Louisiana Commission on the Status of Women, Nov. 1972.

Horner, Matina. "Sex Differences in Achievement Motivation and Performance in Competitive and Non-Competititve Situations." Unpublished Doctoral Dissertation, University of Michigan, 1968. (Article in *Psychology Today*, Vol. 3, No. 6, Nov. 1969.)

Howe, Florence. "Sexual Stereotypes Start Early." *Saturday Review*, October 16, 1971.

————— "The Female Majority" in *Conspiracy of the Young*, Lauter, Paul, and Howe, Florence, eds., New York: World Publishers, 1970, pp. 288-319.

Joffe, Carole. "Sex Role Socialization and the Nursery School: As the Twig is Bent." *Journal of Marriage and the Family*, August 1971, pp. 467-475 (Also in *And Jill Came Tumbling After.)*

Johnson, Laurie Olsen, ed. *Non-Sexist Curricular Materials for Elementary Schools*. Old Westbury, NY: The Feminist Press, 1974.

Kellogg, R.L. "A Direct Approach to Sex Role Identification of School-Related Objects." *Psychological Reports*, Vol. 24, 1969, pp. 839-841.

Kesson, W. "Research in the Psychological Development of Infants: An Overview." *Merrill-Palmer Quarterly*, Vol. 9, No. 2, April 1963.

Key, Mary Ritchie. "Male and Female in Children's Books—Dispelling All Doubts." *American Teacher*, February 1972.

Kirchener, E., and Vondracek, S., "What Do You Want to be When You Grow Up? Vocational Choice in Children Aged Three to Six." Paper presented at the biennial meeting of the Society for Research in Child Development, March 1973. (Also in ERIC, number ED076-244.)

Lakoff, R. *Language and Woman's Place*. New York: Harper & Row, 1975.

Lansky, L.M., and McKay, B. "Sex Role Preference of Kindergarten Males and Females: Some Contradictory Results." *Psychological Reports*, Vol. 13, 1963, pp. 415-421.

Lee, Patrick C. "A Cultural Analysis of Sex Role in the School." *Journal of Teacher Education*, Vol. 26, 1975 Winter, pp. 335-339.

—————. "Reinventing Sex Roles in the Early Childhood Setting." *Childhood Education*, Vol. 52, February 1976, pp. 187-191. (Condensed and reprinted in *The Education Digest*, Vol. 42, No. 1, September 1976, pp. 20-22)

—————, and Gropper, Nancy B. "Sex Role Culture and Educational Practice." *Harvard Educational Review*, Vol. 44, August 1974, pp. 369-410.

—————, and Kedar, Voivodas G. "Sex Role and Pupil Role in Early Childhood Education," in *Current Topics in Early Childhood Education*, Vol. I, L.G. Katz, ed., Norwood, NJ: Ablex Publishing Corporation, 1976.

—————, and Stewart, Robert S., eds. *Sex Differences: Cultural and Developmental Dimensions*. New York: Urizen Books, Inc., 1976.

Lever, Janet. "Sex Differences in the Games Children Play." *Social Problems*, Vol. 23, No. 4, April 1976.

Levine, James A. *Who Will Raise the Children? New Options for Fathers (and Mothers)*. Philadelphia: J.B. Lippincott, 1976.

Liebert, McCall. "Effects of Sex Typed Information on Children's Toy Preferences." *Journal of Genetic Psychology*, Vol. 119, 1971, pp. 133-136.

Lipman-Blumen, Jean. "How Ideology Shapes Women's Lives." *Scientific American*, Jan. 1972.

Maccia, Elizabeth Steiner. *Women and Education*. Springfield, IL: Charles C. Thomas, 1975.

Maccoby, Eleanor E., ed. *The Development of Sex-Role Differences*. Stanford, CA: Stanford University Press, 1966.

———, and Jacklin, Carol Nagy. *Psychology of Sex Differences*. Stanford, CA: Stanford University Press, 1974.

Meade, Marion. "Miss Muffet Must Go: A Mother Fights Back." *Woman's Day*, March 1970.

Miles, Betty. "Harmful Lessons Little Girls Learn in School." *Redbook*, March 1971.

———. "Women's Liberation Comes to Class." *Scholastic Teacher*, Elementary Teachers Edition, November 1971.

Mischel, W. "Sex Typing and Socialization" in *Carmichael's Manual of Child Psychology*, Vol. 2, P.H. Mussen, ed. New York: John Wiley, 1970.

Mitchell, E. "The Learning of Sex Roles Through Toys and Books: A Woman's View." *Young Children*, Vol. 28, 1973, pp. 226-231.

Montemayor, R. "Children's Performance in a Game and Their Attractions to It As a Function of Sex-Typed Labels." *Child Development*, Vol. 45, 1974, pp. 152-156.

Mussen, Paul, and Distler, Luther. "Child Rearing Antecedents of Masculine Identification in Kindergarten Boys." *Child Development*, Vol. 31, No. 1, 1960, pp. 89-100.

Pogrebin, Letty Cottin. "Down With Sexist Upbringing." *MS*, preview issue, Spring 1972.

Ross, Dorothea, and Ross, S. "Resistance by Preschool Boys to Sex-Inappropriate Behavior." *Journal of Educational Psychology*, Vol. 63, 1972, pp. 342-345.

Rossi, A. "Barriers to the Career Choice of Engineering, Medicine or Science Among American Women" in *Women and The Scientific Professions*, J. Mattfield and C. Van Aken, eds. Cambridge: M.I.T. Press, 1965.

Rothbart, M.K., and Maccoby, E.E. "Parents' Differential Reactions to Sons and Daughters." *Journal of Personal and Social Psychology*, Vol. 4, 1966, pp. 237-43.

Rothenberg, Marilyn. "Social and Spatial Organization of Boys and Girls in Open Classrooms." Unpublished doctoral dissertation, C.U.N.Y., Graduate Division, Dept. of Environmental Psychology.

Saario, T.M., Tittle, C.K., and Jacklin, J.N. "Sex Role Stereotyping in the Public Schools." *Harvard Educational Review*, Vol. 43, No. 3, August 1973, pp. 386-416.

Sadker, Myra and David. "Sex Discrimination in the Elementary School." *National Elementary Principal*, October 1972.

Saegert, Susan, and Hart, Roger. "The Development of Environmental Competence in Girls and Boys," in *Women in Society*, P. Burnett, ed., Chicago: Maaroufa Press, in press. (Also available from the authors at CUNY, Graduate School University Center, Department of Environmental Psychology.)

Sargent, Alice G. *Beyond Sex Roles*. New York: West Publishing Company, 1977.

Serbin, L.A., et al. "A Comparison of Teacher Response to the Preacademic and Problem Behavior of Boys and Girls." *Child Development*, Vol. 44, 1973, pp. 796-804.

Sprung, Barbara. *Non-Sexist Education for Young Children: A Practical Guide*. New York: Citation Press, 1975.

Stacey, J., Bereaud, S., and Daniels, J. *And Jill Came Tumbling After: Sexism in American Education*. New York: Dell Publishing Co., 1974.

Stein, A., and Bailey, M.M. "The Socialization of Achievement Orientation in Females." *Psychological Bulletin*, Vol. 80, 1973, pp. 345-366.

———, Pohly, S.R., and Mueller, E. "The Influence of Masculine, Feminine and Neutral Tasks on Children's Achievement Behavior, Expectancies of Success, and Attainment Value." *Child Development*, Vol. 42, 1972, pp. 195-207.

———, and Smithells, J. "Age and Sex Differences in Children's Sex-Role Standards About Achievement." *Developmental Psychology*, Vol. 1, 1969, pp. 252, 259.

S.U.N.Y. State Education Department, Div. of Curriculum Development. *Reviewing the Curriculum for Sexism*, Albany, NY: 1975.

Ward, William. "Variance of Sex Role Preferences Among Boys and Girls." *Psychological Reports*, Vol. 23, 1968, pp. 467-470.

Weitzman, Lenore, et al. "Sex-Role Socialization in Picture Books for Pre-School Children." *American Journal of Sociology*, Vol. 77, No. 6, May 1972, pp. 1125-1150. (Also in *Sexism and Youth*.)

Women on Words and Images. *Dick and Jane as Victims*. Princeton, NJ: 1972, rev. 1976.

———. *Channeling Children*. Princeton, NJ: 1975.

———. *Help Wanted: Sexism in Career Education Materials*. Princeton, NJ: 1975.

Non-Sexist Picture Books for Children

Birnbaum, Al. *Green Eyes*. New York: Western Publishing Co., 1953. All about a cat's first year of life. A story of growth, changing seasons, and history.

Blood, Charles L., and Link, Martin, illustrated by Nancy Winslow Parker. *The Goat in the Rug*. New York: Parents' Magazine Press, 1976. A delightful story of how wool goes from goat to rug, giving a picture of a weaver's skill. The weaver is a Navajo woman who does traditionally valued work. The story needs some editing because there is an unfortunate comment about the women's anglicized name being easier to say than her "Indian" name. Also, the star of the story is really the goat instead of the skillful weaver.

Brenner, Barbara, photographs by George Ancona. *Bodies*. New York: E.P. Dutton, 1973. All kinds of bodies doing all kinds of things. It shows boys and girls in the nude, and on the page showing bodily functions, it has a photo of a small boy on the toilet. A real breakthrough book!

Brownstone, Cecily. *All Kinds of Mothers*. New York: McKay, 1969. An interracial book showing mothers who work both outside and inside the home. The common thread is their love for their children.

Burton, Virginia Lee. *Katy and The Big Snow*. Boston: Houghton Mifflin, 1943. Katy is a tractor who is strong enough to plow out an entire snowed-in city.

Cohen, Miriam, illustrated by Lillian Hoban. *Will I Have a Friend?* New York: Macmillan, 1967. A little boy on his first day at a child care center (taken there by his father) asks if he will find a friend at school. He begins the day feeling uncertain but by the time he leaves, he's found many friends and feels more secure. It shows that boys have feelings of uncertainty and that a father can take part in his child's life.

Ehrlich, Amy, paintings by C.A. Porker. *Zeek Silver Moon*. New York: Dial Press, 1972. This exquisitely illustrated book shows the spontaneous affection and humor between father and child. Zeek's father makes him a cradle and sings him a lullaby he made up.

Eichler, Margrit, illustrated by Bev Magennis. *Martin's Father*. Chapel Hill: Lollipop Power, 1971. This very simple story is about a nurturing father. It shows Martin and his father performing all the housekeeping tasks essential to daily life as well as enjoying play situations together. Although it never specifically states that no mother is present in the family, it can be used as a story with which one-parent children can identify. The fact that the nurturing parent in this case is the father makes this book a fine addition to a non-sexist booklist.

Felt, Sue. *Rosa-Too-Little*. New York: Doubleday, 1950. A story of competence and achievement with a little girl as the main character. Rosa wants a library card and has to learn to write her name to get one. She perseveres all summer in the city, and since Rosa is Hispanic, this has the added attraction of being a success story about a minority child.

Gaeddert, Lou Ann. *Noisy Nancy Norris*. New York: Doubleday, 1965. Nancy is inventive and noisy. She finds out her noisiness is not always appreciated.

————. *Noisy Nancy and Nick*. New York: Doubleday, 1970. Noisy Nancy and her new friend, Nick, explore the noisy city together.

Gauch, Pat, drawings by Shimeon Shemin. *Grandpa & Me*. New York: Coward McCann and Geoghegan, 1972. A young boy recounts his intimacy with his grandpa and their shared love of nature.

Goldreich, Gloria, and Goldreich, Esther. *What Can She Be?* New York: Lothrop, Lee & Shepard, 1972. A veterinarian. Photographs show a female veterinarian taking care of animals in her hospital. Two other "What Can She Be?" books portray the work of a broadcaster and a lawyer.

Goodyear, Carmen. *The Sheep Book*. Chapel Hill: Lollipop Power, 1972. A story of a farmer and *her* sheep. About life and the changing seasons on a California farm.

Grant, Anne, illustrated by Pat Howell. *Danbury's Burning! The Story of Sybil Ludington's Ride*. New York: Henry Z. Walck, 1976. The story of a strong, courageous, and able 16-year-old woman who should be as widely known for her historic ride as Paul Revere. The book is beautifully illustrated in pastel-colored drawings and black-and-white pictures.

Hazen, Nancy. *Grownups Cry, Too*. Chapel Hill: Lollipop Power, 1973. A simple explanation of the kinds of experiences, both sad and happy, that make men and women and boys and girls cry.

Hoban, Lillian. *Arthur's Pen Pal*. New York: Harper & Row, 1976. In this "I Can Read Book" Arthur thinks he would rather be related to his pen pal who can Indian wrestle and do karate than to his little sister who beats him at skip rope. When Arthur discovers who his pen pal is, he learns to appreciate his younger sister, and he learns that rope skipping is a skill too. Arthur and Violet are cared for by a babysitter, a very rare character in children's books.

Kantrowitz, Mildred, illustrated by Nancy Winslow Parker. *Willy Bear*. New York: Parents' Magazine Press, 1976. A little boy works through his anxieties about growing up and his first day of school with his teddy bear. Shows that little boys have fears too and how a stuffed animal can help them resolve these fears.

Kaufman, Joe. *Busy People and How They Do Their Work*. New York: Golden Press, 1973. Although the ratio of jobs is five male and three female, two of the female jobs are non-stereotyped. All of the job descriptions are simple and accurate. While not everything in this book is non-stereotyped, there are pictures of a boy and girl roller skating together, male and female telephone operators, and male and female postal workers.

Klagsbrun, Francine, ed. *Free to Be You and Me*. New York: McGraw-Hill, 1974. While many of the stories may be too old for preschoolers, the book contains the music for all the songs on the record. Young children will also enjoy some of the poems.

Leaf, Munro, illustrated by Robert Lawson. *The Story of Ferdinand*. New York: Viking, 1936. This classic story is about a non-stereotyped bull! He is gentle, quiet, peace loving, and fond of flowers. He does not like to fight, charge, or roar, but he is still a great bull. It is a fine non-sexist book because it subtly criticizes prescribed roles.

Merriam, Eve, illustrated by Beni Montresor. *Mommies at Work*. New York: Knopf, 1961. A good book about mothers who work outside the home. It has a positive tone and combines well the homemaking and working qualities of women. It also depicts many interesting jobs held by women.

———. Illustrated by Harriet Sherman. *Boys & Girls, Girls & Boys*. New York: Holt, Rinehart and Winston, 1972. Though by the same author, this book is not as successful as *Mommies at Work*. It has merit in that it shows boys and girls who are friends with each other; it depicts children of several ethnic groups; and it shows children with a wide variety of interests that are not sex typed. The illustrations are often crowded and confusing, and at times the children are almost grotesque. However, it shows both boys and girls hugging soft toys in bed, catching bugs and worms, and helping with household chores.

Miles, Betty, and Blos, Joan. *Just Think*. New York: Knopf, 1971. Shows mothers who work outside the home, fathers enjoying their children, girls in action, and many other realistic and exciting facts of life.

Newfield, Marcia, illustrated by Diane de Groat. *A Book for Jodan*. New York: Atheneum, 1975. Jodan's mother and father divorce, and Jodan and her mother move away. Her father helps her keep the close relationship they have by making her a book of the things they've shared and his comments to her. A very sensitive treatment of how the separation from a loved one affects children and what can be done to ease the pain.

Pellet, Elizabeth, Osen, Deborah K., and May, Marguerite P. *A Woman is. . . .* 1200 Mount Diablo Blvd., Walnut Creek, CA 94596: Aardvark Media Inc., 1974. This picture book of color photos tells in poetic form what a woman is by describing some of the many roles women fill. Women and girls are pictured as mother, artist, pilot, athlete, and scientist, to mention a few. The last page has blank spaces for the reader to fill in what she or he feels a woman is. There is excellent representation of various racial and ethnic groups, especially the usually absent image of the Asian-American woman.

Reavin, Sam. *Hurrah for Captain Jane*. New York: Parents' Magazine Press, 1971. While in the bathtub, Jane fantasizes about being the first woman captain of an ocean liner.

Schick, Eleanor. *City in the Winter*. New York: Macmillan, 1970. Jimmy stays with his grandma while his mother goes to work. They spend a long snowbound day together doing a variety of things, such as cooking soup, making a barn out of a box, and feeding birds.

Scott, Ann Herbert, drawings by Glo Coalson. *On Mother's Lap*. New York: McGraw-Hill, 1972. A beautifully done picture book for very young children. An Eskimo boy shares his mother's lap with his baby sister and several toys, including his doll.

Sonneborn, Ruth. *I Love Gram*. New York: Viking, 1971. A sensitive story about a young girl's love for her grandmother and her fear and sense of loss when Gram gets sick and is hospitalized. It is also the story of a minority home, headed by a working mother.

Surowieck, Sandra Lucas. *Joshua's Day*. Chapel Hill: Lollipop Power, 1972. Joshua lives in a one-parent home. His mother, who is a photographer, drops him off each morning at a day care center where he interacts with both boys and girls.

Thayer, Jane. *Quiet on Account of Dinosaur*. New York: Morrow, 1964. A fantasy about a little girl who finds a dinosaur on the way to school. She learns so much about dinosaurs that she grows up to be a famous scientist.

Van Woerkom, Dorothy, illustrated by Paul Galdone. *The Queen Who Couldn't Bake Gingerbread*. New York: Knopf, 1975. An amusing retelling of an old German fairy tale. Both the king and the queen learn about choosing a mate for her or his inner qualities rather than looks. They also learn to do for themselves and to be considerate of each other.

Waber, Bernard. *Ira Sleeps Over*. Boston: Houghton Mifflin, 1972. Ira would like to take his teddy bear to his first sleep-over but is afraid his friend will think him a baby. When Reggie takes his teddy bear out of a drawer, Ira goes home (next door) to get his too. Shows that boys also need the comfort of stuffed animals.

Wikland, Ilon. *I Can Help Too!* New York: Random House, 1974. A fine picture book for a toddler, done in durable cardboard with a plastic spiral binding. The toddler, whose sex is not readily identifiable, is shown doing simple chores and activities that a young child of four or five could very successfully carry out.

————. *See What I Can Do!* New York: Random House, 1974. Another Wikland book of the same construction as *I Can Help Too!* The child in this book is about two years old and is pictured carrying out activities appropriate for a child of this age. It highlights activities such as taking off one's socks and using the potty, which is a good way to begin to help children develop a feeling of confidence in their abilities.

Wolde, Gunilla. *Betsy's Baby Brother*. New York: Random House, 1975. Betsy learns what it is like to have a younger brother. Colorful line drawings show baby brother being breast fed and Betsy helping to change his diapers. Little brother is anatomically correct. A positive story of sibling interaction that is real and natural.

———. *This Is Betsy*. New York: Random House, 1975. The first of the Betsy books, which introduces the reader to a little girl much like the ones found in anyone's family. Tells about the times when Betsy is acting according to adult expectations and the other times when she's doing what she really wants to do.

———. *Tommy Goes to the Doctor*. Boston: Houghton Mifflin, 1972. Tommy does to his teddy bear what his doctor (a woman) does to him.

———. *Tommy and Sarah Dress Up*. Boston: Houghton Mifflin, 1972. Two very young friends have a fine time dressing up and trying on both male and female clothing.

Yashima, Taro. *Crow Boy*. New York: Viking, 1955. Another classic children's book, which belongs on every non-sexist list. *Crow Boy* deals with the feelings of a young boy, a subject not usually dealt with in stories for young children. Chibi is the butt of all the class jokes for six years in elementary school until a male teacher takes the time to discover his uniqueness as a person. By letting Chibi display his unusual talent, he helps the children to realize that they never bothered to find out what kind of person Chibi was, just because he was a little different. A further asset of *Crow Boy* as a non-sexist book is that it is set in another culture, rural Japan. It also teaches the appreciation of differences. Best for children five years and older.

Young, Miriam. *Jellybeans for Breakfast*. New York: Parents' Magazine Press, 1968. Two little girls imagine all the fantastic things they will do some day, including going to the moon.

Zolotow, Charlotte, pictures by Ben Schecter. *The Summer Night*. New York: Harper & Row, 1974. A gentle story of a nurturing father and his little girl. When she can't go to sleep on a warm summer night, her dad figures out all sorts of ways they can enjoy themselves.

———, illustrated by William Pene Du Bois. *William's Doll*. New York: Harper & Row, 1972. This well-written book is outstanding for both the quality of its language and its message. It is about a boy who wants a doll to nurture and the reactions of his family and friends to his request. When his grandmother explains to William's father her reason for buying William the doll he wants, she gives a moving account of the importance of the development of gentle and nurturing qualities in prospective fathers.